How I Earned the Ruptured Duck
From Brooklyn to Berchtesgaden in World War II

Joseph G. Dawson III, *General Editor*
Editorial Board
Robert Doughty
Brian Linn
Craig Symonds
Robert Wooster

How I Earned the Ruptured Duck

From Brooklyn to Berchtesgaden in World War II

LEO BOGART

Foreword by Charles Winick

Texas A&M
University Press
College Station

Copyright © 2004 by Leo Bogart
Manufactured in the United States of America
All rights reserved
First edition

The paper used in this book meets the minimum requirements
of the American National Standard for Permanence
of Paper for Printed Library Materials, Z39.48-1984.
Binding materials have been chosen for durability.

Library of Congress Cataloging-in-Publication Data

Bogart, Leo.
How I earned the ruptured duck : from Brooklyn to Berchtesgaden in World War II / Leo Bogart ;
foreword by Charles Winick.— 1st ed.
p. cm. — (Texas A&M University military history series ; no. 92)
Includes index.
ISBN 1-58544-299-2 (cloth : alk. paper)
1. Bogart, Leo.   2. World War, 1939–1945—Personal narratives, American.
3. Soldiers—United States—Biography.   4. World War, 1939–1945—Campaigns—Western
Front—Personal narratives.   I. Title.   II. Series : Texas A & M University military
history series ; 92.

D811.B57865 A3 2003
940.54'8173—dc21

2003007370

For Nick
Whose story is a sequel
to this one

Contents

List of Illustrations / ix
Foreword by Charles Winick / xi
Preface / xiii
1. Preliminaries / 3
2. Training for War / 13
3. Military Academia / 26
4. Preparing to Go Over There / 34
5. The Theater of War / 41
6. On the Continent / 60
7. On the Heels of the Wehrmacht / 65
8. The Chateau / 73
9. The Discovery of Germany / 88
10. A Postwar Assignment / 118
Afterword / 141
Notes / 143
Index / 147

Illustrations

RMS *Queen Mary* / 42
The Chateau de la Commanderie at Fouron St. Pierre / 75
A mixed crew between shifts at the Chateau, 1944 / 75
The center of Verviers in the 1920s / 77
In newly liberated Venlo, 1945, the author with Edward Du Bois / 98
Striking a pose at a German tank trap on the Siegfried Line / 99

Maps

Western Europe / 44
Benelux: Belgium, the Netherlands, and Luxembourg / 45

Foreword

This is a remarkable book, largely based on letters written during World War II to family and friends by a young soldier who later became one of the country's most distinguished social scientists. We follow him from pre-enlistment life to a varied military career, overseas service, and discharge in 1946.

Leo Bogart's story is noteworthy because of the wide scope of the author's adventures and the warmth and acuity of his writing, which reflects a novelistic sensibility and a thoughtful and articulate observer. The book provides the texture of a novel that has a range of settings, situations, and fascinating characters. There is a momentum in the style that partially derives from the material having been written simultaneously with or just after something had happened, rather than recalled years later.

The author had just graduated from college and could not only speak French and German but was extremely well informed about art and music. During his military service, he visited sites relevant to the arts with the zest that characterized everything he did.

Some settings and situations that have figured in other war memoirs appear, but they are presented with a freshness that makes us feel that we are hearing about them for the first time. Thus, there are foreign language specialists who do not speak the language, incomplete or incomprehensible orders, the chow line with no chow, basic training, landing in France, V-1 buzz bombs, techniques of goldbricking, troopship life aboard the *Queen Mary*, visits to Picasso, and daily life in a military government office.

The heart of the book is the way in which a very keen observer, although only in his early twenties, feels and thinks his way through the most important four years of his life in a series of very unfamiliar settings. His perceptions and reactions are set forth movingly, seriously, and wittily.

Bogart writes with understatement. The most critical decision of his military career, in which he decides to volunteer for flying duty that would involve his listening for enemy signal communications in the lead plane of a bomber formation, gets only a few paragraphs. He volunteered even though a waiver for a vision problem was required, and he knew that the assignment was dangerous. He simply notes that "I had to subordinate myself to the larger objective." He was not chosen for the assignment, but he notes that a friend who was selected was shot down and killed. The matter is not mentioned again.

He also writes with an eye for the illuminating and apt detail. Commenting on a Luxembourg prison town, he describes ". . . the lively streets of a town full of black-stockinged young matrons wheeling clean pink babies in perambulators, brisk, clean-shaven businessmen wearing black homburg hats and briefcases, pretty girls and kids on bicycles—the busy bourgeois world of buy and sell and go to church that goes on and on through war and peace and fall of governments. But here in the depths of the prison was the ugly core on which all the tranquility falsely rested."

Probably the most extensive discussion in the book deals with Bogart's reactions to and interactions with Germans, both soldiers and civilians. He agrees with a Dutch soldier that the American treatment of the conquered Germans has already (in 1945) been too humane, yet Americans will never avoid being humane. He speculates about the impact of the Nazi corruption of the German mind. He presents vignettes of many Germans and displaced persons whom he meets and with whom he converses. These experiences probably contributed to his later writing the first scholarly analysis of attitudes toward the Holocaust as a graduate thesis at the University of Chicago.

Rick Atkinson, who has published several books on the history of World War II, has said that the U.S. archives of the war weigh over 14,000 tons. As a veteran of World War II who contributed to that tonnage as a staff member of the army's Historical Division, I believe that Leo Bogart's report on his experience brings the many dimensions of the war to life better than any archival-based report ever could. I cannot recall a more interesting and evocative memoir of a young man's military experience. This book is a gem.

Charles Winick
Professor Emeritus of Sociology
City University of New York
Lieutenant Colonel, U.S. Army (Ret.)

Preface

> There are but few important events in the affairs of men brought about by their own choice.
> —Ulysses S. Grant, Preface to *Personal Memoirs*

> Professor, which came first, World War One or World War Two? I always forget.
> —An undergraduate

As a small boy in the late 1920s, I watched a Memorial Day parade of World War I veterans, many of whom, marching briskly, were still able to squeeze into their old uniforms. They were followed by a small, slow-moving contingent of veterans of the Spanish American War, some erect, some with canes, a few in wheelchairs. At the end of the procession, in a flag-draped open cabriolet limousine, rode two ancient survivors of the Civil War, perhaps in their last parade. Thus all wars and those who bear witness to them pass into history, surviving in artifacts, images, and documents, but no longer in living memories.

Wars represent compelling and transformative *personal* experiences for the participants, but only in the cases of the Civil War and the Second World War was participation a near-universal *national* experience. To say this is not to minimize the searing impact of the Korean and Vietnam wars for those who served in them. It is merely a reminder of the reality that at stake in World War II, as in the Civil War, was national survival. These two great wars of the nineteenth and twentieth centuries engaged the entire society, brought whole generations into military service, and had cataclysmic social consequences.

The Second World War has been much celebrated in fiction, especially in filmed fiction that demands perilous exploits, death-defying bravery, and incessant action. But much of war involves inaction and boredom. Wartime events are characterized by stupid error as well as by intrepid ingenuity.

I lost cherished friends in World War II, that most necessary war, but I was fortunate. I did not flounder in muddy foxholes, advance against the rattle of machine guns, or bare my bayonet in hand-to-hand combat with battle-hardened adversaries. But my military experience was not atypical. Of the sixteen million men and 200,000 women who served in the U.S. armed forces during the Second World War, only a minority ever came under enemy fire, and an even smaller percentage were in actual combat.[1]

What all those sixteen million shared was an uprooting, a sense that our private worlds would never again be the same, an appreciation of our mortality. The war was a time for introspection even as it also opened up new worlds and brought new acquaintances.

Fiction demands a plot, and non-fiction a theme, but life follows neither structure. This book traces my coming of age (I was twenty when I entered the army) and the steps in my continuing education (though unlike Henry Adams, I do not propose to step back periodically to remind the reader whenever a new lesson has sunk in).

Any visit to the past entails pauses at critical junctions. At every fork in the road a traveler may take one direction and not another after conscious deliberation and choice; the path may merely follow random chance; or it may be imposed by external forces. Such forces, blind and unpredictable, abound in wartime and in the workings of military bureaucracy. My own adventures illustrate how the haphazard workings of fate interact with personal decisions and make the sum total of any life unique and unpredictable.

My four years in the army were devoid of heroism or drama, but they shaped me more intensely than the events of any comparable period of time before or after. I recorded many of my experiences in the letters assembled in this volume, which vary in tone because they were sent to different people. Much was left out because of censorship or a lack of time, so I have filled in the gaps with additional reminiscences. (These are set in a different type font, except for some explanatory phrases I have placed within brackets in the text of the original letters. Necessarily, my retrospective recollections lack the freshness and immediacy of the day-to-day reports to my correspondents, but some of them reflect intense experiences that remain sharply burnished in my memory. I have refrained, however, from the memoirist's common temptation to reconstruct long-past conversations and to embroider dimly recalled details.) I have excised irrelevant material from the letters, but have included some sophomoric political observations and aesthetic judgments that reflect my juvenile outlook. I have also retained a few references to friends and acquaintances from my college years, since they represented the links to my earlier, smaller world, from which the war separated me for good.

Military service requires submission to an all-embracing environment, but it does not entail an abandonment of previous ties, interests, or identity. My letters reflect the continuing tug of my previous associations and concerns, as well as my curiosity about the new civilian scenes to which the army introduced me. The war engaged me, as it did many others, long before I put on a uniform. It confronted me with a continually changing cast of characters and a succession of dazzling touristic impressions. It led me, after a period of transition from civilian life, to a series of peculiar confrontations with the vast military institution, to the battle for Europe, and finally to troubling confrontations with the defeated enemy.

The war was an overwhelming presence in American life, and in my own, long before I was caught up in it. This book begins some months after Pearl Harbor, with a description of the setting from which I entered the Army Signal Corps' enlisted reserve. I was employed in a factory that made military equipment for shipment to our new ally, the Soviet Union, and thus had a fresh perspective on some bizarre happenings on what was called "the home front." Once I was inducted into active duty, my journey followed a capricious path, which landed me back in college as a member of the Army Specialized Training Program. The ASTP at its peak that year placed about 150,000 enlisted men in universities for training that was intended to help increase manpower in professional specialties that were in short supply. It put me on a course that led to an assignment in signal intelligence. This brought me, after a stay in England, to Omaha Beach (several months after D-Day) and, after vicissitudes, through Germany. A new job in military intelligence was cut short by a near-fatal accident.

That is the bare outline of my military career and of this book. Though my letters tell of the day-to-day events (or at least, of those that I could write about), their chief interest, some sixty years later, is probably in the subjective feelings they convey.

The terrorist attacks of September 11, 2001, have made Americans suddenly aware of their direct vulnerability to dark forces at loose in remote parts of the globe. The destruction of the World Trade Center's twin towers demonstrated the fragility of the landmarks on which we all depend to guide us in our daily lives. As a soldier in Europe I saw that the Europeans had already absorbed this disorienting lesson. Much of this book records its troubling reverberations for me.

Throughout my overseas adventures, my facility with French and German, and occasionally my nodding acquaintance with Russian, made it possible for me to communicate directly with people wherever I went and heightened my sensitivity to the agonies that war brought into ordinary lives.[2] (My language skills were acquired in an immigrant household in which my parents switched seamlessly between German and Russian. My mother came from a small-town German-speaking family in the imperial Russian province of Courland, now Latvia. My father was from the Russian-speaking city of Odessa [now in Ukraine] and had studied at the Technical University in Munich.)

I have divided my letters and fresh comments under chapter headings, but the divisions are arbitrary. Precisely because life moves on from hour to hour and day by day, this running record illuminates some small homely aspects of the Second World War that cannot be found in military histories that describe the marshalling of forces, the capture of cities, and the casualty counts.

How I Earned the Ruptured Duck

Chapter 1

Preliminaries

A short-arm inspection initiated my army experience. A line of us, stripped to our shorts, were ordered to drop them and present our penises for review by a physician adept at detection of chancres and lesions. Shown in rich colors, these sores were featured in numerous films that warned us, in the next four years, to beware of the dangers of venereal disease and unprotected sexual intercourse. The physical examination, in the red-brick army-recruitment building facing New York's Battery Park, followed my enlistment in the spring of 1942.

I was entering the Enlisted Reserve Corps, which deferred my entrance into active duty for about six months, while I completed a cram course on the fundamentals of radio. Its purpose was to provide the Army Signal Corps with technically trained officer material. The course itself was conducted every weekday evening at Hunter College in Manhattan. My fellow-students had been lured, like me, by the prospect of a commission and by the temporary prolongation of our civilian existences. Many of them were lawyers; the incongruity between their meager abilities and their apparent success in civilian life led me to ask one of the more intelligent among them how they ever managed to win a case. He explained that when they appeared in court, they merely had to face each other.

I had graduated from Brooklyn College the preceding June and was living in Flatbush with my parents, sleeping in the living room with my younger brother on an extensible couch. I had just landed a job at the Pilot Radio Company, in a decrepit loft building in Long Island City, an hour and a half commute each way. It occurred to me vaguely that my radio studies might fit in with my work as secretary to the chief engineer, but I would already be exhausted at the end of the work day, when I took the subway from Queens to Manhattan, and ready for sleep when my classes ended and I headed back for Brooklyn, with several changes of trains.

My view of the war was confused and ambivalent and had undergone a series of vacillations. At the age of eight, I had been assured by my mother that there would be no more wars; they had just been outlawed by the Kellogg Briand peace pact of 1929. A few years later I was devouring a series of library books about

"The Boy Allies"; they featured the fictional exploits of a group of American teenagers who performed miraculously heroic feats in the First World War.

The gory images of war must have a grim fascination for the adolescent mind. In my high-school library I pored over illustrated histories of the World War and of the Civil War, and studied the names and tactics of generals and the progress of battles. But war had come closer to home than the picture books. It had brought my parents together and had forced them to flee Bolshevik Russia.

In the 1930s, the legends of "the Great War" were being deflated. The bright radical students whom I admired in high school "knew" that the atrocity stories were created by Allied propaganda, and that the war had nothing to do with Wilsonian ideals of democracy and everything to do with the division of the world's spoils among rival capitalist cabals.[1] The best proof of this lay in the inertia of the western powers when Fascist Germany and Italy overwhelmed the Spanish republic. The posters and songs of the Loyalists were the political talismans of my contemporaries. *"No pasarán!"* "They shall not pass," the slogan of the International Brigades in the Battle of Madrid was our own rallying cry. I took the fall of Barcelona to Franco's forces as a hard personal blow.

The campus scene at Brooklyn College, which I entered just before my sixteenth birthday in the fall of 1937, was one of frenetic political engagement, set off by the continuing Depression and by the conflicts in Europe and the Far East. Activist student groups and their faculty allies voiced every possible variant of opinion on the left side of the ideological spectrum. Among these factions, the Communists (financed by Moscow, as was later proven) were the best organized and the most visible. Under the banner of the American League Against War and Fascism, they carried a large train of fellow travelers in their wake, all joined in the demand for a Popular Front in the western democracies. The Molotov–von Ribbentrop Pact in 1939 opened the way for the German invasion of Poland. The anti-war American League changed its name to the American League for Peace and Democracy, and the Communists joined with other leftists and with a curious assortment of traditional isolationists, right-wingers, and Fascist sympathizers in assailing the "imperialist war."

I was tossed about in the maelstrom of conflicting and changing politics, in which feelings about the war in Western Europe were confused by a host of domestic issues. Our campus newspaper, the *Vanguard*, was produced cheaply in a shop in Manhattan's printing district. One of the printers had served in an Italian troop unit that had participated in the never-ending battles on the Western Front in France. His frightening descriptions of bloody trench warfare tilted me toward pacifism. I wrote editorials opposing the war and the proposed establishment of a unit of the Reserve Officers Training Corps (ROTC). But while I thus adhered to the conventional radical politics of my college generation, I was dismayed by the Leninist tactics of the Young Communists and upset by the fall of France.

I used my press pass to get into a movie theater in Yorkville that showed the Nazi propaganda films *Feldzug nach Polen (Campaign in Poland)* and *Sieg im Westen (Victory in the West*, which depicted the fall of France and the Low Countries).[2] These films conveyed the impression of a war machine endowed with almost supernatural powers, crushing even the mightiest opposition. German warriors were proud, confident, and superbly equipped. The message was reinforced by cheerful mailings from the German Information Office in Washington, which came to me weekly at the *Vanguard*. I described my mood in a letter to a high school classmate who had gone on to a Midwestern university:

May, 1941:[3] It will all make wonderful reading in the psychology textbooks of a saner world (when one finally materializes, in several millennia or so)—war neuroses, lassitude, demoralization, etc. etc. etc. People just don't give a damn about anything any more. And I—I give a damn about everything, and that's the trouble with me. It isn't just *Weltschmerz* [world-weariness] or over-aged adolescent despondency. It's something that's got everybody down. Let me construct a metaphor: we're sitting in a dentist's waiting room. (We envision the ultimate pain). We're at the end of a tremendously long line that doesn't seem to get shorter. And we wait and wait and wait and look at each other surreptitiously and pore through the old magazines that fail to interest us, but nothing is happening. We've waited too long now to go away; we've got to stick it out.

I'm really afraid I've become a cynic. I have no faith in this crusade for democracy, but I don't want Hitler to win. I am fed up with the only radicals who have been doing anything—the Communists. Russia seems to be shot to pieces and ready to do almost anything to save her skin. The May Day parade this year was a puny spectacle.[4] (I saw the Nazi picture, "Sieg im Westen," the one they used to soften up Balkan diplomats before they marched in. It's horribly marvelous. On a field with cows still innocently grazing on it, tanks battle in fantastically tangled disarray like miniature electric cars in a Coney Island amusement park, running every which way and bumping into each other.)

At a national meeting of student leaders, held at Rutgers University, I was shaken by a stirring call for American intervention on the allied side. The speaker's logic was irrefutable, his passion infectious. Afterwards I followed him to the New Brunswick railroad station and queried him mercilessly until his train came. He was the theologian Reinhold Niebuhr, and he had disturbed my cherished convictions.

The ambiguities ended shortly after my college graduation in the spring of

1941, when Hitler launched his invasion of the Soviet Union and the Communists transformed their cry, "The Yanks are *not* coming!" into "The Yanks are not coming too late!"

Pilot Radio

Getting a job was not easy at a time when the country was still slowly emerging from the Depression and unemployment was still high. It was especially difficult for anyone who had registered for the draft and whose future was uncertain. While I looked for full-time work I was employed part-time as the research assistant to a former professor, the Dutch art historian Leo Balet, who was editing a new *Dictionary of the Arts*. My task was to examine all the entries pertaining to art in a wide range of encyclopedias in various languages, to make sure that nothing would be missing in our own publication.

This academic exercise in the great reading room of the New York Public Library contrasted sharply with my new job at the Pilot Radio Corporation. My pay soared from fifty cents an hour to twenty dollars a week. More to the point, I was briefly introduced to two aspects of the war that I would never have encountered in my army service: the pressure and occasional corruption of domestic defense industry and the Soviet military.

When I started working there, Pilot Radio had largely converted from the production of consumer goods. It had received a large contract from the War Department to manufacture portable radio transmitter-receivers (named RV-3, for Radio Victory) for use by troops in the field; these were destined to be shipped to the Red Army under the lend-lease military aid program. A small laboratory was dedicated to the design of television receivers for the postwar era. Its little group of engineers lived in a world apart, shunning any contact with the dismal apparatus of the assembly line, where hundreds of workers assembled, connected, and soldered equipment through several shifts each day.

By contrast, L. C. Shapiro, the Chief Engineer, was a man deeply committed to every phase of the project, rushing down from his office to the factory floor to solve problems, fretting over the delayed arrival of parts from suppliers, drumming his fingers impatiently, and working long hours in his driven dedication to the task.

June 2, 1942: The Chief Engineer's office has been removed from the noisy nexus of the plant (The Kremlin) to the more secluded but also much more sooty atmosphere of the penthouse (High Tor). Through the large windows in front of me I see the chimneys and gas tanks of Long Island City, the Neo-Gothic towers of Queensboro Bridge, and the Manhattan skyline, all heavily obscured by grey rain.

L. C.'s sidekick was Abe Schneiderman, a genial giant of coarse habits, heroic sexual exploits (according to his own account), and an incredible familiarity with the serial number of every one of the thousands of resistors, coils, screws, brackets, vacuum tubes, and other elements that went into the appliances the factory was churning out. It was he who rejected my first expense account, showing me how to rewrite it to include "miscellaneous expenses," non-existent taxi fares, and other items that swelled the modest total by at least 20 percent.

The expenses were incurred on an overnight sleeping car trip to Washington. I undertook this in connection with an instruction book prepared for the field transmitters being shipped to the Russians. I was given this assignment as a result of my familiarity with the Cyrillic alphabet, my rudimentary Russian, and my friendship with the Red Army engineer, Lt. Aleksander Konstantinovich (Sasha) Godzevsky, who had been sent over to check out the equipment before it was shipped through the submarine-infested North Atlantic to Murmansk.

The Russians

Godzevsky, then in his mid-thirties, was from Leningrad (now again St. Petersburg) and had been engaged during the early 1930s in the monstrous collectivization of the rural Ukraine (of which he spoke proudly). His wife, still in the Soviet Union, wrote to him of the horrors of the German invasion. She had witnessed an episode in which people had been forced into a building, which then was set afire. As Sasha sat at his work station at the end of the Pilot assembly line, he would half-sing half-hum American popular tunes, the words enunciated carefully in a strong Russian accent: "Somebodiy's rucking my drimbut."

Hardly any English at all was spoken by Sasha's superior, Gen. Fyodor Ivanovich Belov, who occasionally showed up from the Soviet military mission in Washington. I was fascinated by the apparent gap between Belov's exalted military rank and his outwardly undistinguished intellect. In Washington I once found him studying a weeks-old issue of *Pravda*, on whose front page appeared the photograph of a robust, kerchiefed young woman heroically screwing a tailfin to a bomb. *"Zamechatelnaya dievushka!"* (splendid girl!) he exclaimed lustfully, and then repeated this several times. He was tall, slender, courtly, and affable, and it was obvious that he spent most of his time signing papers that he had not read. But he had survived the purges of senior officers through which Stalin had almost destroyed the effectiveness of the Red Army in the few years before the start of Operation Barbarossa.[5] Like Godzevsky, he always wore civilian clothing.

Amtorg, the Soviet foreign-trade organization, was the clearing house for Lend-Lease aid, and a hub for Soviet espionage, although this was not apparent at the time, to me or anyone else. I made several visits to their office off Union

Square. It was headed by a grim, unsmiling, and charmless tough named Korovin, an archetypal Soviet apparatchik who favored fedora hats. The liaison with Pilot Radio was a small bespectacled personage who looked like a female version of one of Disney's seven dwarfs. She spoke fluent English with an accent not perceptibly different from what was then current on the Lower East Side. She offered strong opinions on American politics, referring to the Congress, dominated by Republicans and Southern Democrats, as a "Nazi Congress," which I took to be permissible exaggeration.

The Chief Engineer

December 20, 1942: Last week my boss said to me, "Leo, when are you going into the Army?" "Oh, the end of January," said I. "Well," said he, "I'm thinking maybe we don't want to let you go into the Army." "It's too late," said I, "You can't defer someone who's already inducted." "That's all right. We'll go to the provost-marshal," said he. At that moment there was given to me sudden understanding of how ridiculous it would be for me *not* to go into the Army, how necessary and vital would be for me the military life, even in the company of the five-dollar-bill-matching gamblers of my Hunter College course.

Dear brother IG (IG are the initials of the head of Pilot Radio, Mr. Isidor Goldberg, who has lifted himself by his bootstraps and has never let go of his bootstraps and whose perspectives are appropriately deformed) embodies [the worst of] capitalism, with its corruption, its inequity, its distortion and waste of fine human beings, and worst of all, its apparent impermeability. The other day I had a long talk with my boss, an extremely intelligent and able man with a fine sense of humor (the social kind) beneath a gruff veneer that terrifies most of his underlings. I complained to him of IG's treatment of his serfs and me in particular.

Now the CE [chief engineer] ordinarily speaks of IG as "the head of the company," speaks of private enterprise as an eternal truth and inspiration, and skimps and saves on nickels and dimes when these belong to the company. When I spoke to him he just sighed bitterly, broke down and told me that he too was gypped and exploited and lied to, but that he couldn't stand up and fight for his men or himself, or the best interests of production and the war, because he was deathly afraid of being kicked out on his ass if he did. Afraid not only of losing his job but of not being able to get another. Maybe you belong in a big corporation or in government, I suggested. No good. He had worked in both for many years, and everywhere he had found the same suppression of his engineering talent (which I genuinely admire) to work on research problems of his own choosing for the benefit of mankind. And he can see no scheme of reference outside of his own pocket. He says, if Hitler wins the war he's right. If we win the war, democracy's right. Which at least follows logically from his more local rationalizations.

Intellectuals are in a very peculiarly fortunate position. Even if nobody prints their books, they can go on writing them anyway provided they've got a small teaching job to take care of their bread. An engineer or worker has nothing, nothing outside of the work itself.

Into this sickly beehive of honeyed filth Tovarishch Alexander Konstantinovich Godzevsky walks like a carefree demigod. No one can offend him, because his government pays the bill and within certain limits he can speak his mind. To anyone brought up in the West, with all the prejudices and neuroses of the West circulating in his psychic stream, AKG is like a man from the moon. Completely aside from the fact that he is an intelligent, sensitive and warmhearted human being, his reactions, even in the small things, are marked by a sense of social responsibility that I have never seen in anyone else I have ever met.

Mr. IG has brought in his half-brother, recently returned from exploitation of the Brazilian peons, to be chief spy at Pilot. [Since there could only be one Mr. Goldberg in the company, the brother was known as "Mr. E. Manuel." This brought a fresh complication; there was already another Emanuel Goldberg (a cousin) on the premises. He was henceforth identified as "Mr. Manny."]

The brother Goldberg unctuously introduced the cousin Goldberg to Godzevsky, who turned into an enormous mountain of clear white ice, slowly but surely freezing the insincere insipid exploiter smiles of the brother and cousin Goldbergs.

Little Albert, the little lame draftsman, quit his $20 a week job to go somewhere else, leaving our drafting department shorthanded at its busiest moment. Trialogue: LB: "It's just damn tough that we have to be undermanned right now." The Brother G: "Well, what happened to Little Albert?" LB: "He left for another job." TBG: "Why did he do that?" AKG: "Because he was underpaid. That's why. Because almost all the people who work at Pilot Radio are underpaid." TBG (chuckling): "Haw haw haw!" Godzevsky again becomes an iceberg. White jagged ice flames dart from his arctic bulk, scattering shit and derision at his oncoming pursuers. LB too becomes a little iceberg, with streaks of earth and dung and granite in it, and a family of seals cavorting on top.

December 29, 1942: The sound of whirring generators and electric erasers and elevators fills the air with electrical vibrations of varying cyclical frequency and amplitude of vibration. At any moment now the door may open and the bossbrother (Mr. E. Manuel) may introduce his false smile and heavily perfumed head with a cheery "Good morning Leo. How are you coming on that list of assembly numbers?" To which I shall reply in my own cheery way, "Why I'm working on it right now."

Coming to work this morning, with the soft rain falling on the nocturnal *niaiserie* [silliness] of the Avenue J [subway] station I found the ghostly figure of

Chester Kallman [a college friend, poet, opera librettist and long-time companion of W. H. Auden], holding his worldly goods in a paper bag of indescribable origins. He is on his way to Michigan after a two-day stay in the bars of the Village, and informs me that he will remain in Michigan and grind lenses after he gets his M.A. in January.

Socialist Realism

January 12, 1943: Last week I went to Washington on business for dear old Pilot Radio. In the National Gallery there is an El Greco painting of an old bearded literary saint [St. Jerome] writing theological poetry in his chocolate-brown-woodwork and scarlet-satin-upholstered study that is just sublime. And roomfuls of marvelous Rembrandts so vital and intense that you can't but feel that they were painted by a contemporary who had read Freud and Proust and been expelled from the Communist Party.

In Washington I stayed with Sasha Godzevsky and his friend Alyosha Dubinin. On several occasions I treated General Belov to dinner (at Pilot Radio's expense) and I worked by day in the offices of the Soviet Purchasing Commission. Sasha and Alyosha share a bachelor apartment in the suburbs, in a "Model Home" variety of apartment house three stories high. They don't have much furniture. What they have they bought helter-skelter and it is the Gimbel's Basement variety. There is a bookcase with the plays of Eugene O'Neill, some other decent literature, some Pocket Book detective stories, some copies of *Life* and a few technical books on radio—all in English. On the walls there are a few tiny and uninteresting Japanese watercolors, relics of the trip here, and a tremendous *1941* calendar with a lush pink nude leering at the visitor continuously as he moves about the room. There is a record player–radio with a medium-size collection of records, mostly Tchaikovsky program music and other Russian late 19th century romantic stuff, with one Red Army chorus record, a lot of crappy American jazz and some operatic airs. (Of Gigli, G. says, "He is a Fascist, but what a wonderful voice!"[6])

G. on Art: I went to the museum with him and his girl friend (an OPA [Office of Price Administration] stenog—a blonde with a low-cut dress and soft correct affected speech). [I was shocked to hear Godzevsky's aesthetic views. He had been raised on Socialist Realism.] G. on the marvelous French Impressionist collection: "They all look as though someone had made a perfectly good painting and then let it stand for a week in a vat of gray water so that everything is blurred and faded." On a vivid Cézanne still-life: "How many people have already painted the same oranges and the same lemons and here he hasn't even made them look like the real thing!" On a brilliant cynical Toulouse-Lautrec painting of a death's headed ballerina with pale green skin: "Who ever saw a woman with such a face, and with green skin?"

He was unmoved by my explanation that the artist was trying to tell us something through his color scheme. I suggested that it might be necessary, to understand and appreciate these things, to know something of the artists who painted them and of the social conditions out of which the works came. "Ah, then you have to be very clever to know everything about any piece of art you might ever see. But a poor stupid person like me just has to keep on never liking the right things." I dropped the discussion there, particularly after he said, "You should see some of *our* art!"

This cultural aridity on the part of an intelligent person is quite frightening. One is also inclined to draw all kinds of negative conclusions from it until one remembers that my good and intelligent friends, the engineers of Pilot Radio, would react in almost the same way to the same paintings. The grotesque aesthetic of materialism nurtured by the Soviet intellectual regime is very little different from that which the Western bourgeoisie maintains for its own dogma and that of the masses whose opinions it fabricates.

One point I have never seriously considered was made very clear by my contact with these Russians. When we think of our American bolos [Bolsheviks, i.e. Communists] we think unconsciously of a compact group of individuals whose characters fall within certain comparatively narrow limits of background, intelligence, education, frustration and protoneurotic personality traits. Therefore when we think of Russian bolos we unconsciously list them within the same personality category. We don't fully realize that when an entire great nation accepts, lives and grows by a set of revolutionary social principles, its component individuals cannot become mechanical and similar like the members of a small zealot band; they will continue to be as diverse in character and way of thought, as universally human and tolerant as any other enormous and unselected group of people. This variety is an enormous factor in determining the practical day-to-day political standards of the Soviet Union (which is almost always in the Russian as well as English conversation of the Russians I met "Russia" and not "the Soviet Union.") My discussion with them of problems such as the postwar disposition of Germany provoked opinions as different as any group of comparable Americans would offer. Their ideas in that particular regard, incidentally, run along very practical and conservative, though humane, lines.

PM [a short-lived radical daily that carried no advertising and was subvened by Marshall Field] ran a symposium on the subject which I made Godzevsky and General Belov read. Dorothy Thompson vaguely suggested that in the postwar world outstanding members of the younger generation of European countries should be inculcated with the principles of justice and truth (as expounded by Dorothy Thompson) in schools of leadership established by the United Nations.[7]

Belov, who is a conservative middle-aged gentleman, all scrubbed and clean and rosy-pink, with [rimless] pince-nez of course, beamed. "Ochen Khorosho!"

[Very good!] G. disagreed. "That's nothing but Fascism! To take people of different nationalities and cultures and make them all try to think in exactly the same way—that is what Hitler does with the Germans!" Of Cecil Brown's proposal that all Nazis responsible for criminal acts outside the bounds of "legitimate" warfare be executed[8]—whether they number "one million or five million," G. exclaimed, "The man is an idiot! Does he know what that means—to kill a million people?" What makes this position worthy of interest is that not an American unaffected by the war is talking, but a Russian. Two nights earlier G. had told me—and he is from Leningrad—that one million people died of starvation in that city last winter; and the daily stories of unimaginably horrible German atrocities which fill columns and columns of the Russian press daily have only one meaning, he says: "Kill!"

These people are fundamentally and thoroughly tolerant and democratic. They take for granted attitudes that the enlightened among us manage to acquire only with difficulty and incompletely. When they deal with little-minded American business men their smallest conflict over petty contractual haggling assumes shades of meaning that are tremendous and dramatic. You have already heard of Isidor Goldberg and his numerous relations. The latest of these is his cousin, Max Goldberg of Servwell Press, who was brought in to be a consultant in the printing of the instruction book (which is being handled by the Russians).

His services were to consist of taking the finished copy from my hands and placing it in those of the actual printer, Futuro, who ordinarily handles Russian instruction book jobs for Amtorg. For a half-hour's work, which could very easily be performed by me or one of the other fellows here (choosing paper stock), he was to get 10% of an order worth $7500. I had told my Russian friends about it; they are paying for it and are entitled to know.

The other night I was at Amtorg with Max Goldberg, and the Russians sprang a beautiful trap. For an hour and a half we sat in the acre-large plush and Morocco [leather] office of Mr. Korovin, the vice president of Amtorg, while he delivered thunderous and sly ultimata, threatening not to help Pilot at all on the book unless the order were delivered through them. Poor M.G. was shitting in his pants. Korovin is an impresario, with a brilliant sense of dramatic humor. Imagine what you or I could do as the head of a purchasing corporation with limitless resources and with every capitalist entering my office as a supplicant. What a marvelous opportunity to play Satan! Korovin does it with relish and extraordinary aptitude. Every word, every thought-sequence in this closet conflict was loaded with unconscious implications of the larger and irreconcilable struggle between human orders based on greed and on use respectively.

Russia is socialist Russia, a foreign nation and not Russia the seat of the world revolution. The Comintern is [regarded as] a despised tool, the foreign admirers are poor pawns.

Chapter 2

Training for War

With my radio course completed, my transfer to active duty took place almost immediately. Like all recruits, I was reconfigured out of my civilian existence, probed, tested, trained, indoctrinated, and tossed about from one installation to another.

Leo Balet, my revered art history professor, had been a museum curator in Germany before the First World War. Though he was Dutch, as a civil servant, he had been drafted into the German army and had served in Carpathia on the Russian front. He lived in an apartment with handsome black contemporary furniture and no single object of art marring the stark white walls. His bald head was freshly shaven each morning by his worshipful wife. He spoke on any subject with great precision and assuredness.

Balet responded to my apprehensions about putting on the uniform: "You vill laugh as you have never laughed before in your life!" That was true, but it wasn't the whole truth.

Fort Dix

Fort Dix, New Jersey, was a reception center for new troops. One fellow enlistee showed up in his uniform from the previous war, complete with puttees, which were no longer in style.

February, 1943: I left Pilot Radio a few days before I came here, with mutual good will, and the admonition of the great G. that I return to his fold after the war. The good boys there bought me a good toilet kit and drank my health in my cheap wine.

Fort Dix, February 2, 1943: I have completed the processing which makes a soldier out of an ordinary Leo Bogart; that is, I have acquired a uniform and an insurance policy, and undergone various aptitude tests, the standard personnel interview, and the set of anti-tetanus and anti-typhoid inoculations that are known ominously as "the Hook." There is quite a legend here about "the Hook." Once you have survived the ordeal you are entitled to yell at all the un-uniformed jeeps, "Watch the Hook! Oh, those propellers!" Actually, the needling leaves your shoulder sore for a day or two, but it's really nothing.

The clothing process is very interesting. You enter the large warehouse dressed in your civilian clothes and carrying one of your two duffle bags. You take off all your clothing and put it into your bag. All your body measurements—head, neck, chest, waist, arms, legs—are taken. The first thing you are given is long woolen underwear, which you put on. Next two pairs of summer pants, then two pairs of regular wool pants. And so on through fatigue uniforms, field jackets, caps, hankies, shoes, coat, until you leave the building completely clothed, with the heavy bag weighing you down.

Fort Dix, February 3, 1943: It is now 6 o'clock and I have just finished a day of the Army's most dreaded detail—KP or Kitchen Police. Each company of about 800 men has its own mess hall, with a staff of about twenty Negro cooks. Each day a group of about 50 men is assigned to help out with all the miscellaneous dirty work. I was awakened at 4:45 this morning and stopped work about half an hour ago. My duties were fairly typical. I stood in the cafeteria line handing out bread, helped carry into the storeroom sacks of onions, barrels of hams and the frozen carcasses of cows. I scrubbed the storeroom shelves, brushed and mopped the floor, handed canned supplies to the kitchen, scrubbed the potato peeling machine, peeled onions by hand, helped hash potatoes and scrubbed one of the enormous kettles used for cooking. To show you how big it is, it took more than an hour and half to clean it.

February 4, 1943: Another typical Fort Dix day. It's about 2:30 P.M. and I expect to be "working" for another hour or so. I am sitting comfortably in a warehouse writing letters. Every hour or hour and a half a truck comes around and we load it with crates of canteen covers for about 20 minutes. Then I sit down again and return to my letters and the other fellows sit around and do nothing, which is what the average soldier does with all his free time. It's raining outside and the snow-covered landscape is dreary and flat, but with a certain soft ghostly charm. Our barracks is a two-story wooden building, each floor of which has 25 doubledeck beds. The beds must be made in a devious special way. Our first sergeant (the legendary Lajdek, whose face resembles that of Popeye the Sailor Man, though he lacks any of Popeye's endearing qualities) is a particularly darling man, even though he is illiterate and has the intelligence of a 3-year old child. He greets all cowering offenders with the same reproach (in a heavy Polish accent): "You no soldier! You SHIT!! I'll burn your ass!" He calls to the assembled ranks: "You college boys, fall out to the right! All right, you carry in the beds. High school graduates, fall out to the left! You carry in the mattresses! And the rest of you dumb bastards, stand by and see if you can learn something!"

My hands still smell of onions from yesterday's KP. All this smells of war only in the vaguest and most preliminary way. Practically nobody reads the newspapers, and politics is an unmentionable subject.

February 9, 1943: We were rooted at random out of the barracks at 7:00 A.M.—10 of us—lined up outside in the darkness, and sent marching to an unknown destination. I had a sudden intuition of what a Gestapo victim feels—helplessness, questioning, a sense of rage at the sheer illogical injustice of the procedure. We worked in the records office, scrubbing the floor all too briefly, and then rubber-stamping insurance forms with the name and rank of the officer in charge, who spent the day sitting at his desk with his head buried in his hands. When we finished the morning's work we were told to report back after mess, at 1:00 P.M. At 12:00 we had an early formation and fell out as "Special Duty Men." "All right, report back to [building] T-19!" said the sergeant. So the 10 of us started marching back in formation, discussing the fact that we still had a free hour left. "Let's fall out and come back at 1:00," I suggested, and each of the ten men present made a similar remark. As individuals we were all completely in agreement. Still as we discussed the situation we kept marching in formation to T-19, dominated by some mysterious collective military *id*, formed after only a few days of military life.

So the mechanization has already begun. The whole thing is fantastically ludicrous—the incredibly foul-mouthed perverted terrorists who are our non-coms; the soldiers who laugh at the guy who reads the newspaper, who read comic books in the Service Club at night and lie blankly on their bunks at day, who ride each other on wheelbarrows, emitting the noises of choo-choo trains; the frightful wastage—of food, of time, of human energy and self-respect; and the beautifully brutal, haphazard rationality with which the whole thing is organized—like the games of early adolescent kids! Anyone who takes this seriously is bound to be miserable. But the whole thing has the elements of a colossal joke. If one once understands and accepts this, adjustment is not only easy, but actually pleasurable.

The past eleven days have been vastly rich in sociological experiences. I love being outdoors in the fresh cold country air; I like the rabbits I saw in the woods yesterday as we hiked through the Fort Dix roads; I like the completely solid dark dreamless sleep which chops me out of the world for 8 hours each day; I like the plenitude of sloppy spicy food. (If it's too revolting I just don't eat it.) I like my long good conversations with my new friends, three boys from the other section of my despised Hunter radio course whom I discovered here to be fine, bright and stimulating (one a successful lawyer, another an ex-*PM* reporter, a third a Communist saddle manufacturer with a thriving absentee business); I like the enormous amount of free time I have up here—enormous by contrast with the many horrendous days spent between 6:45 A.M. and 11:30 P.M. in subway, Pilot Radio and school; I like learning about people as I am learning here.

Bert Morton [another college friend who later became an expatriate in Majorca and an acolyte of Robert Graves] looks exactly like a German Stalingrad prisoner, and his psychic state is also similar. His nose is red and swollen and perpetually draining snot. His lower lip is always jutting forward, revealing his front teeth. He appears to be developing a hunchback. When one of the fellows asked him what he did in civilian life he lowered his eyelashes shyly and said, "I'm a poet!" He doesn't talk or laugh or sing or do anything much but blow his nose. He is unfortunately possessed of an overly sensitive soul. As for me, I shall never renounce loud gleeful laughter or fierce hatred of commonly accepted evil. I am very very sure that I belong in this war, and in this army, and I can't imagine any other place to be.

Fort Dix, February 10, 1943: Yesterday some of the boys dug ditches, which they had to fill in as soon as they were dug. I worked for half an hour in a warehouse, took an hour out walking around the grounds on the pretext of visiting the latrine and then went on a nice truck ride.

February 15, 1943: We're leaving this afternoon for an unknown destination. You can be quite sure that I'll be quite happy wherever I go, since my friends will be with me, and Army life, at least as far as I've known it thus far, is very peaceful and restful. A small group of us had by the close of our stay here developed the art of "goldbricking"—avoiding unpleasant duty—to a high degree of perfection. Whenever we were sent in a long column to the warehouse, for instance, we wormed our way to the end of the ranks and then marched away in another direction at great speed. The problem then arose of where to safely enjoy our leisure. Often, when it was nice, we went for bird walks around the neighborhood. We were never stopped, since we always looked as though we were on some important business. Once or twice, when it was raining, we went into the movies, which play perpetually to entering "jeeps," educational films showing that espionage and sex do not pay. Yesterday we discovered an attic in the Recreation Hall where Ossy Renardy, the famous concert violinist, who is a private here, was practicing. Poor Renardy was trying very hard to play his intricate exercises while around him carpenters were sawing and hammering and a radio was blathering in a nasal woman's voice.

Another refuge at Fort Dix was the band headquarters. One of our friends, a big, bald fat lawyer named Teiger, decided that to avoid unpleasant duties he would become a cymbal player in the band, and he quickly became a cymbal virtuoso, though he had never seen the instrument before. Another fellow who played the piano declared he performed on the glockenspiel and was given that job. The band quarters are hilarious. No one knows how to play except the trumpet and clarinet men and one of the five drummers, and the resulting cacophony is terrific. Teiger puts the sheet music in front of him very seriously, and every once in a while he clashes his cymbals together gaily. None of the players knows what is going on. "All right, when I say '3' we start," says the band sergeant. "1, 2!" "What are we going to play?" the players ask. It doesn't make much difference, because everything sounds alike anyway.

Camp Crowder, Missouri, February 17, 1943: Camp Crowder is a kind of heaven compared to Fort Dix. We eat like gentlemen from dishes instead of from sloppy cafeteria trays. The officers and non-coms speak like human beings instead of like ogres. While you eat you hear the news and soft music. Now, how do we get to this blissful place from Fort Dix? We stand in the rain for two hours, march through the rain carrying our two Army packs, are herded into an ordinary coach railroad car and ride for 56 hours through the sub-zero weather of the Midwest. The steam pipes freeze. There is no heat, no water to wash with; the toilets are clogged up and unusable. One tries to sleep but can't because the card players yell too loudly. We pass through Pittsburgh, Fort Wayne, Chicago, Kansas City, but can't see anything because the shades are drawn and we can't leave the car during the journey. When the train stops at a station, the ice on top of the car melts and drips all over the people inside. Locomotive soot covers everything in the car. People spit in the aisles. Result—a mild case of measles, which is keeping me confined in the hospital for a seven-day quarantine.

Basic Training

I arrived at Camp Crowder for Signal Corps basic training with a high fever that earned the Army's omnibus diagnosis, *nasopharyngitis*, which covered everything from a mild cold to double-pneumonia. In my case, there were also small red spots.

February 22, 1943: I haven't been bored or unhappy here in the hospital at all. This measles ward most of the time seems more like an insane asylum than anything else. No one is sick for more than a day or two and after that there is very little for all these healthy young men to do for the rest of the 7-day quarantine except to lie in bed and read or do nothing. So every once in a while they go wild. Just now, for instance, someone had an apple left over from breakfast and started to play ball with it. It almost hit the nurse when she came in, and splattered against the wall over her head. The nurses here aren't very much to look at, but when a nice-looking one comes in occasionally, the entire ward starts to groan and moan in unison to arouse sympathy. At night after the lights are out the acrobats get to work. This is a one-story building, so the ceiling is crisscrossed with beams that hold up the sloping roof. Shouting Tarzan cries, the boys bounce on the beds until they can jump up and catch hold of a beam. Then they swing along the ceiling, from hand to hand, emitting fierce jungle yells, until they can drop on the laps of their unsuspecting enemies.

March, 1943: The radio course I took apparently means nothing to the Signal Corps. I have been pre-assigned to Message Center [School], which is about the best thing I could have gotten. After 6 weeks I can apply for Officer Candidates School. Judging from what I have seen of the officers here and their work it almost seems preferable to remain an enlisted man with a good technician's rating that carries more pay and more interesting work than a second lieutenant's.

During our basic training at Camp Crowder, reveille was followed shortly by an assembly and roll-call, after which virtually everyone retired to his cot for a snooze before the bugle sounded chow call and we marched off to breakfast. Loudspeakers throughout the camp blared appropriately martial music. There was a continual sound of marching feet and of the chants which were intended to boost our morale: From the non-commissioned officer in charge: "Sound off!" From the obedient soldiery: "One, two." "Sound off!" "Three, four."

We stood in formation at repeated intervals during the day, usually at attention, sometimes "at ease." When the order, "Company dismissed!" was given, there was a loud expressionless murmur: "Hubba hubba hubba." But this mysterious and universally used mantra had other uses. It was applied with a strong inflection on the first syllable as an expression of delight over the promise of some rare special treat or the presence of comely females.

March 5, 1943: Our rifles only weigh 8 pounds, but double in weight every 30 seconds that they're held. We have already crawled on our bellies across an imitation battlefield.

March 8, 1943: Tonight we're not going to scrub the barracks. For a change, we're going to be bawled out and reinstructed in how to fold blankets for airing, and how to make the loop sling for the rifle. How our day is spent? We got up at 5:15 as usual, scrubbed the place so that any part of it could be eaten from, ate breakfast (bacon, eggs, cereal, bread, butter, milk, coffee, orange, potatoes), went for several hours' lecture on rifle practice, spent a few more hours on the range shooting dummy ammunition at the roaring cold wind, marched back for lunch (roast beef, cabbage, potatoes, bean soup, bread, butter, celery, apple pie, lemonade), went out on the range again all afternoon, took a half-hour of exercise and went back to eat supper (hamburgers, rice, relish, lettuce, candied carrots, chicken soup, bread, butter, apricots, coffee).

March 11, 1943: Last night we went on a patrolling expedition to capture a "machine gun nest" in "enemy" territory.

If homosexuality existed in the wartime army it was kept very much under wraps. I only encountered signs of it once. At Camp Crowder, a small corporal who worked as a clerk in the training company's office received a peremptory and dishonorable discharge. He was called in to the company commander, shorn of his two pitiful stripes, and sent on his way. His final salute to the commanding officer was delivered with elegant precision. He was the only member of the permanent cadre who had ever behaved in a friendly and civilized manner to us recruits.

The Ozarks

I had never been farther south or west than Washington, D.C., and the discovery of the Ozarks was a revelation. Camp Crowder was outside the small city of Neosho, Missouri, which then had a population of eight thousand. The nearest metropolis was Joplin, which had about thirty thousand, and to which we naturally gravitated. I had my first exposure to the sign, "Colored Seat to Rear" in every public vehicle, and always went to the back of the bus throughout my sojourn in the South.

April, 1943: The dry flattened earth resounds to our footsteps, the ground is crushed by the tremor of our marching feet. How many are there marching, crushing the hard sod, disrobing the calm cool earth, trampling on the grass, smelling the sweet air, ignoring the red dawn and the bird's trill and the distant roars of sound that are not sound but the nameless essence of wartime spring? Yes, on moves the war, the all-embracing, the final and common denominator. Will there be other springs, we wonder. The grass, how green it is!

For its training exercises, the army had taken over a huge tract of farm and woodland and evacuated the inhabitants. I was shocked by the tiny, spare, and dilapidated sharecropper shacks in which large families had lived. The interior walls were insulated with layers of newspapers, which served as wallpaper too. I had in all the depths of New York's dreary Depression never seen evidence of such hideous poverty.

March 21, 1943: Yesterday I went with my friends Bert Morton and Joe Miller to Carthage, a little town of about 15,000 people some 26 miles away from here. There are some horrible slums, completely unlike anything I've ever seen up North. The streets end abruptly and become unpaved dusty roads lined with tumble-down wooden shacks, pigsty size, with scraggly yards that hold babies, chickens, pigs, goats, cows, and pheasants in completely helter-skelter profusion. We also passed the local jail, erected in 1872 and still in use. It's an ugly concrete building with sides all full of iron bars and poor prisoners (you can just imagine the balls and chains on their legs) looking forlornly out of the windows. The people are all very friendly to us soldiers. Everyone you pass on the street says "Hello" or "Howdy" or "Wonderful weather we're having."

I applied for admittance to the Army Specialized Training Program (ASTP), which had been set up ostensibly to provide the army with specialists who were in short supply. (A secondary purpose may have been political: to shore up the country's colleges and universities, which had lost a substantial chunk of their student bodies to military service.) The ASTP provided pre-medical, pre-dental, and engineering training for men who had not finished college, and had also set up programs in psychology and in foreign areas and languages, to produce specialists for intelligence, military liaison, and military government duties.

April, 1943: Today I was interviewed by a Lt. Col., a Captain and a First Lt. on the ASTP. They are not interested in men who have already completed college, but they are putting my name on a long list of eligibles. I was recommended in Electrical Engineering, in which I am not at all interested.

In the meantime, I received training in the use of the army's high-tech communications methods:

April 12, 1943: On Saturday we had our pigeon instruction, attaching messages to the birds' legs, releasing them, and visiting their lofts.

April 14, 1943: The instructors often take half the period calling the roll. We already practice Message Center work in a big building divided into rooms connected by "radio" and "telegraph" facilities (phones, actually), which we pretend are miles apart. The object of our training is to make us expert in as many things as possible. I have been a chief, clerk, dispatcher, radio operator, code clerk, messenger, switchboard operator, etc. Tonight I went to see a USO show—pretty good except for a nasty crack about Brooklyn (which pretty generally means Jewish in the Army) and a sympathetically comic imitation of the Fascist murderer Mussolini.

April, 1943: Except for the typewriting, I find Message Center School quite interesting. We study subjects as varied as cryptography and the uniforms of the Japanese Army.
   If I complete this course with excellent grades (and I see no reason why I

shouldn't) I may be made a Message Center Chief with a Master Sergeant's rating—and that is a very good job indeed. This afternoon I spent taking a three hour examination for the Army Specialized Training Program, which is sending soldiers back to college.

April 19, 1943: Neosho is very depressing. A complete small town with nothing in it but soldiers. Sunday morning at 7:30 we went to Carthage, and Bert Morton and I walked out into the country, which was rolling and very lovely. We passed a lot of farms and finally came to a tremendous mansion and estate by the side of the road, with a beautiful lawn shaded by trees. We asked the caretaker's permission to lie down on the lawn. After a pleasant hour of dozing he invited us in for chicken dinner with himself, wife, sister and sister-in-law—really good, simple, reactionary, religious Negro-hating Middle Western farmers who offered a 5-minute long grace before eating, referring to us "blessed boys" as messengers from God to their "humble table."

April, 1943: As I look back on basic [training] now I realize that it wasn't at all strenuous, but the pressure of always having something to do made the month a tough one. I don't have any illusions about what's ahead. Things are going to get tougher—not easier—and I'm not interested in a soft job even if I could get one, which is very unlikely. The war to destroy Fascism isn't going to be won at Camp Crowder.

May 17, 1943: This weekend was spent very pleasantly in Joplin with my friend Joe Cream. We were introduced to two teachers of music at Kansas State Teachers' College, one a pleasant young man who plays the piano and has a fine record collection, the other (Miss Hesselberg) a Russian Jewish lady of about 55, who lives with her sister of about the same age, who is a doctor. They are from Orel, lived in Moscow and Odessa, studied at Berlin, speak German beautifully, are the friends of [pianist Artur] Rubinstein and [Russian bass singer Fyodor] Chaliapin and the aunts of [the film star] Melvyn Douglas, make brilliant witty conversation, play the violin marvelously, and fed us prodigiously on tea with rum and lemon, blintzes with pot cheese, and cherry jam.

May, 1943: Here I am sitting in the record room of the Joplin USO listening to Mozart's G Minor symphony. I'm all alone here. In the whole building there aren't more than three or four soldiers. Only a little while ago I was in the stockyards about 4 miles outside of Joplin, attending the weekly cattle auction. Farmers and their women, looking like animated bits of earth, wearing every imaginable rural costume, ranging from railwaymen's caps and overalls to ten gallon hats, green flannel shirts and high-heeled riding shoes. The stock (pigs, horses, cows, mules, sheep) is in pens where prospective buyers can examine it. The actual auctioning takes place in a small arena. We sit in the ringside seats, the animal is led into the ring, the auctioneer begins to howl his unintelligible gibberish. The farmers sitting on the inside of the ring have canes with which they whack the beast to keep it on the run. Pigs average $30 apiece, cows $100. The crowd treats the whole thing like a kind of circus. The kids run through the aisles, everyone spits out tobacco, gossips, eats sandwiches, and has a good time.

The price for today's blissful freedom was last night's duty as night fireman. I tended 6 furnaces and 5 boiler ovens from 4:30 p.m. to 5:30 a.m., with only a few random hours of rest. It was a pretty terrific job, but today was well worth it.

Since urban pavements were my natural habitat, my encounters with the natural world left me rhapsodic.

May, 1943: Now I am in the stockyards at Joplin amidst a strange rural gaiety as alien to me as the ritual of an obscure foreign tribe. How can these people be, I wonder, and what is my connection with them? Yet I pass among them not as a stranger but as a brother and friend, and the kids salute me with grave precision. There is a strength in the people and a joy in the land. How great and beautiful it is, how perfect are the shapes of natural things, the stalks of wild grass and the trim green of tended summer lawns, the stately glory of trees and subtle efficiency of insect structures, how raw and beautiful the bright blues and reds and yellows of forest flowers and the wings of the wild birds calling in the scented fields! And the eternal kaleidoscope of clouds and sky, shuffled by the endless Midwest winds.

And in all the fabulous richness of the land, whence come the frightening hovels, the rural slums, the ragged barefoot kids, the pallor of poverty in the faces of the folk? And in the towns of America the constant reminder of home's gentility—the rows of solid white houses with the green lawns and the flower beds, the pretty little girls jumping rope and the pretty little boys on their tricycles, the sun on the clean pavement mellowed by the sheltering trees. And each town with its own small gossip and politics, the many who like to be where they are or pretend, and the few who hate it and are caught by it. My sweet unmarried lady of late middle age, the former student of Joachim, who stands in her brown bricabrac bourgeois parlor and raises from her violin the tremulous soaring souls of the musical great, as she plays she cries. To be away from here, from this sordid little city, from the insensitivity and silly greed of it, the piddling lust to be greatest and best and first in things inconsequential and even so beyond reach.

After all this how eery the return to the ghostly camp, the orderly row of white barracks, the powdered rigor of commands. The war, the army proceed in strange and illogical ways. A composite of human frailty, and yet the huge mass of us will overwhelm the foe, with the incredible power in our lavish food and equipment. It is a war without anger, a war in resignation. But war must always be like that, mustn't it? I have had a vision of the whole process, out on the make-believe battlefield. Away up on the next hill there is a human being holding a rifle with which he intends to kill you. You don't bother to consider his immortal soul, or that he is a bearer of the Fascist cancer. He is a small black point, a target like the targets on the rifle range, and you, being a good soldier, squeeze her off easy [the standard training instruction phrase for shooting] thinking only of the mark and not at all of the cause for which you fire at it. Then, as the comic corrective to all bad thoughts of war, there is the Saturday afternoon parade and the dogs yelping and barking happily in front of the inspecting officers. The band sounds its traditional fanfares and the show goes on.

May 22, 1943: Just now the mousey corporal up front is going over the same cryptography lesson that we've had for the last three days. Some of the fellows are sleeping. Others are reading the paper.

May, 1943: The Saturday after next I will complete my Message Center School course. Several days after that I will be shipped to one of two places: (1) a tactical unit or regular military organization, or (2) more probably I will be sent to the Central Signal Corps Training Center, in another part of Camp Crowder.

I am sure you are all very much concerned to know why I am still a buck private. The stories that I and every other ERC [Enlisted Reserve Corps] man was told regarding immediate commissions, high ratings, etc. are so much crap. No one in the Signal Corps or anywhere else in the Army is any longer commissioned except after graduating from Officer Candidates School. Apparently because the high moguls feel that the war will be over in a year or two, OCS in Signal Corps is being pared to the bone and may be eliminated by October. There is now such a plenitude of officers that there is one for every 15 men.

May 25, 1943: Last night I was invited over to visit my old ladies in Joplin and there met the charming family of a colonel at Camp Crowder, which included two lovely daughters. I made quite a hit with the whole bunch and was asked to come over some time. Now, when I'm just on the verge of departure!

My application to enter the ASTP now underwent a strange series of turns. Those applicants who met the minimum AGCT (Army General Classification Test, essentially a measure of intelligence) and educational achievement standards were given yet another test to determine their fitness for this highly selective program.

Those who had cleared all the hurdles (I was one of them) were placed on a list, but this list turned out to be too small for the army to meet its commitment to the universities. The military's creative solution was to set up a second list made up of those who had flunked the test. Those lucky enough to be on it were exempted from active overseas assignments, while the unfortunate few who had made the first list were still being called up and shipped out to the South Pacific, the Aleutians, and other interesting places. If this was an injustice, the army had an expression for it: "Tough shit!"

My social contact with the colonel had led me to assume that there might be some faint flicker of rationality among the higher authorities and emboldened me and my friend, Joe Cream, to pay a visit to the Post chaplain, who said he would look into it. Apparently he did, because a few days later the original orders were revised to exclude those men who had not yet reached their twenty-second birthday. (It was assumed that they did not yet have college degrees, were therefore educationally malleable, and could be refitted as engineers or physicians.) The hapless Joe, who was about thirty, was soon on his way to the Pacific Theater of War, where he earned a commission in the Signal Corps; he stayed on in the peacetime army.

May 27, 1943: Again the irrational Army has done the unexpected. I had already been given my aluminum canteen and was all set to hand in some of my clothing and get my steel helmet and blankets, when I was notified today that I have been scratched from the shipping list.

May 28, 1943: The curious operations of fate turn my Army career into a ridiculous procedure. I can now tell you that the tactical unit I was slated to join is leaving directly for somewhere in the South Pacific. I was scheduled to leave today, then scratched. I wrote you about how I went out into the field every day and lay in the meadows reading Balzac. Unfortunately I was apprehended, and yesterday found myself in the kitchen scrubbing pots for Message Center Field Problem, for the very troop train on which I was originally scheduled to leave. When I returned to my company after this trying day I discovered my name on the duty roster for company KP today and table waiter tomorrow. So at 5:30 this morning I reported sadly to the mess hall. At 9 o'clock I was yanked out of the kitchen and told that I am shipping tomorrow to the University of Nebraska. Everything from now on, as hitherto, is chance and luck. As the colonel I met last week told me, if our ERC group had entered the Army just a few months before it actually did, our commissions would have been a practical certainty.

KP was always irksome, but doing the pots and pans was a particularly doleful task. One mess officer criticized my technique. He yelled, "I want the water to be so boiling hot you can't put your hands in it!" leaving me with the intriguing problem of how to scrub the pots I couldn't reach. On one occasion a fellow sufferer insisted on mopping the floor with his fly open and his genitals protruding. When the mess sergeant ordered him to button up (this was before zippers) he retorted, "You make me work like a horse; I might as well look like a horse."

Chapter 3

Military Academia

I was one of a fortunate few whose army career included a happy interlude of campus life, and one of the fortunate fewer of these who were not subsequently thrust into the most intimate perils of combat. The best part of this continuing education was not in the classroom, but in my exposure to unfamiliar regions of the United States. The University of Nebraska had been designated as a central facility to test and assign soldiers to other universities in the ASTP.

Lincoln, Nebraska, June, 1943: Everything is a little fabulous, because at this moment I should really be on my way to a port of embarkation along with the rest of the boys from my message center section. I was saved simply by the fact that I haven't yet reached my 22nd birthday.

We left Camp Crowder yesterday afternoon after a 4 hour wait at the railroad station. We were given free candy bars (courtesy of Baby Ruth Inc.) and the camp band was on hand to see us off. I wasn't sorry to leave, but Camp Crowder is really a very nice place. We came here by Pullman, ate dinner in the diner. Our quarters here are in a brand new library [Love Library, mirth-provokingly named after a Mr. Love], the study halls of which have been made into dormitories. Our beds are made with two sheets instead of one—indescribable luxury! My bed is right next to a window, with a lovely tree and grass view. The meals here—if the first two are any criterion—are unbelievably magnificent. [This obsession with food may be due to the fact that my family had spent most of the 1930's first on relief (now called welfare) and then with my father on the meager payroll of the Works Progress Administration.]

Just now I'm sitting in the Student Union music room, which has a colossal record collection. Later I shall go swimming in the university pool. I hate to revel in all this when my buddies are on their way to fight the Japs, but I can't help feeling elated, with Smetana, Bach and Sibelius bellowing at me. I am obsessed with the feeling that my presence here is obscene and wrong. I belong now where the war is going on, not in the safe sanctuary of a Midwestern college. (The radio is now blaring forth the merits of Johnny Goodman's Athlete's Foot Remedy, cost

$2, presenting a program of state news and views by Charles A. Quinn in the interests of good government.) This war is the biggest thing that my generation will experience, and I want a full measure of that experience.

The sightseeing highlight of my stay in Lincoln was a guided tour of the state capitol, home of Nebraska's unique unicameral legislature. The guide was a short elderly compulsive talker who was no admirer of New Deal deficit spending. After every stop on the tour he would conclude his description with the slowly and solemnly enunciated phrase, "And it's *all* paid for!" He ended with the solemn recitation of a poem of his own composition whose final lines have reverberated through the years: "And by the living God I say, no red flag will fly over this fair land of mine, unless it has some white and some blue in it too!"

June 7, 1943: Last night one of our boys came in drunk, leaving a trail of feces from one end of the dorm to the other. Life is funny.

Since I was already a college graduate, the engineering and pre-med programs were ruled out for me, and I was pointed toward the Foreign Area and Language program.

June 8, 1943: Yesterday [after taking a series of language tests] I was told that I had been accepted in four categories: French, German, Spanish and Russian.

June 14, 1943: Nothing happens in this madhouse except madness. Just now the latest vogue is fencing. Little men with foils and masks cavort merrily about our beds slashing at each other and wreaking havoc in their wake.

June 22, 1943: I was just told that I am leaving tomorrow morning for the ASTP unit at Vanderbilt University, Nashville.

I had selected Russian as the language I wanted to study, and Vanderbilt offered the designated course. I was sent off with my travel orders on a long and circuitous train ride, via Chicago, in the company of Bob Carlson, affable, highly intelligent, apple-cheeked, and red-headed (though his hairline was already receding). Carlson was from Erie, where his father and brothers were employed by General Electric. He had just graduated from the University of Pittsburgh, and the only language he had ever studied was Latin. Why he elected to study Russian as his only modern language is still unclear both to him and to me. (The Army eventually trained him to break Japanese codes, but he never put that skill to work.) Our travel orders placed *me* in command of our two-man troop movement, because B comes before C.

Nashville

June 25, 1943: I am quartered in a room about 12' square, 2 windows, a table, 2 chairs, one dresser and a combination wardrobe and dresser. There are two double-decker beds. One is empty. The lighting is quite poor. The dormitory building (Kissam Hall) is an old brick horror dating back to 1900. The only consoling factors are that we have a toilet right next door and the mattresses are 8" thick.

June 28, 1943: Our trip here was comparatively pleasant. We [Carlson and I] had an air-conditioned streamliner from Lincoln to Chicago and had about one free hour there. The U.S.O. is fabulous.[1] They've taken whole hotels over for the pleasure of the servicemen, and you can get a complete meal free there. We got the last available Pullman tickets from Chicago to Nashville. I share my dorm room with Carlson and a boy named Garrison Mitchell from Arkansas.

No one knows anything about a Russian class. They are going to try to make us study German or French. Everything is completely botched up in the regular G.I. way.

A two-hour-a-week Russian class eventually did materialize, taught by a German instructor whose familiarity with the language was probably less than my own, and who struggled to keep up with his students. I elected French as my principal language of study. Under the tutelage of Monsieur Rochedieu, who had come to the United States long ago to avoid his Swiss military service, we explicated texts and sang *Auprès de ma blonde* as well as French nursery songs like *Frère Jacques*, which had no erotic overtones. The rest of the time was devoted to a potpourri of lessons in European history, social structure, and government, taught by professors who ranged upward from incompetence and were supplemented by occasional guest lecturers. There was a periodic military drill to remind us that we were in the service after all.

June 7, 1945 [to my parents]: I now raise a delicate point. In the last two months I've been paid $15 and I'm not on the present payroll either. Moreover life in a city is about 5 times as expensive as life at camp. So please send me a postal money order for $10 to last me until I get paid in a few weeks, because I've only got $3 now.

July, 1943: I got paid yesterday. It was pay day for the whole army and downtown Nashville last night was simply indescribable. There are about 30 soldiers for every civilian and most of them have nothing to do except to get mildly drunk. It's very lively and nonetheless depressing.

July 21, 1943: About my program, here goes: Military training—5 hours/week; Gym—3 2-hour periods. 4 hrs. in sociology and geography of Central Europe; 4 hrs. in economic background of Central Europe. French—12 hours; German—1 hour; Modern history—4 hrs. (This course is a complete waste of time; the instructor is a moron. Otherwise the instructors are quite good.) [Bypassing military channels, several of us went to Dean Donald Davidson to complain about the offending instructor, who confounded Yugoslavia with Czechoslovakia. He was actually fired.]

As far as I know most of the regular students here are pretty dumb and that is why the teachers love us so.

Vanderbilt's civilian students were largely housed in sorority and fraternity houses that ringed the campus. This was a world of their own into which few of us entered. A minority of "independents" represented the free spirits who welcomed our presence. The nearby Peabody College campus overflowed with pretty Southern belles. There were occasional manifestations of traditional regional hospitality on Sunday afternoons—church picnics featuring luscious servings of fried chicken and corn bread.

The commandant of our ASTP unit was a college professor in civilian life, so the military exigencies of our existence were kept to a minimum. We did a certain amount of drill, and on one memorable occasion we performed a field exercise and stormed the full-scale sandstone reproduction of the Parthenon that symbolizes Nashville's claim to be "the Athens of the South."

Academically, we had scant contact with Vanderbilt's distinguished English faculty, which spearheaded the literary Southern Agrarian Revival movement. Our sociological instruction (presumably valuable for our future role as Europe's military governors) was provided by a corpulent Dickensian character named Weyland B. Hayes, who expounded to us the Booker T. Washington "separate but equal" doctrine, extending the fingers of one hand to demonstrate the metaphor, though it was apparent that no two fingers were of equal length. Our contingent of Communists, Socialists, and other Yankee left-wingers listened politely but mockingly to this nonsense.

The most brilliant of the Communists was Danny Lehrman, a graduate of City College who had, he told me, the second highest I.Q. in the U.S. Army. Lehrman was pear-shaped and walked with an ungainly and decidedly unmilitary waddle. He was filled with endless supplies of nervous intellectual energy which he dedicated to the pursuit of a never-fulfilled career as a natural scientist. (After the war's end he pursued his research into animal behavior, but died after only a few years.) We debated endlessly. I was shocked by his defense of Lysenko (a fraud who was Stalin's favorite agronomist); in spite of his brilliance he was a doctrinaire true believer. Lehrman's side-kick was rotund, perpetually smiling, usually silent Harry Yoselowitz, in civilian life a clerk in the nether levels of New York City's municipal court system.

For me the Civil War was ancient history, commemorated in the cross-hatched illustrations of the picture books I had devoured in the high-school library. It was a revelation to discover how vivid and fresh that war was in the sensibilities of all the Southerners I encountered. Whether they referred to us Northerners as "damnyankees" or hid behind a cultivated veneer of civility, they were almost without exception strongly conscious of their separateness, and suffused with a collective sadness and resentment over the defeat of the Confederacy. Amidst the generally unquestioning acceptance of segregation and racial bigotry, there were some free, dissenting spirits in the university and in the Methodist churches. They had to be sought out.

July 25, 1943: I just returned from a 3-hour bus ride to Monteagle, Tennessee, a little town in the Cumberland Mountains about eighty miles away from here on the Chattanooga road. The Highlander Folk School, located in a farm house in the hills near there, is the center of the Southern labor movement. The mountains are lovely, but the soil and the people who cultivate it are very very poor. They live in horrible shacks and log cabins as bad as or worse than anything I saw in the Ozarks. The school is trying to get these people to improve their condition, but tradition and prejudice are strong enough to make that a very big job. There were some very interesting people up there, and I met a cousin of [Texas Congressman] Martin Dies [chairman of the House committee on un-American activities] who calls him a fascist.

At Highlander I met Jim Dombrowski, a slender, bespectacled, and impressive labor organizer with a deceptively laid-back and folksy manner that disguised his courage, energy, and will. "When real change comes to this country," he told me, "the South will be leading it. We've been so far behind that there's a radical streak that will find its way out."

On Saturday nights, downtown Nashville filled up with folk from the Tennessee countryside. They gravitated toward the city's main square, where the men squatted on their haunches, spat tobacco, and stared at each other and at the passers-by. On a side street, the shingle outside a doctor's office bore his name and the all-encompassing title, "SPECIALIST." The Ryman auditorium housed the Grand Ole Op'ry, whose main attraction was a youthful Roy Acuff, in the flower of his remarkable career as a country-music singer. In the heat, which rose to well over 100 degrees, the audience swayed in time with the music and rhythmically beat the air with their fans, all emblazoned with Acuff's smiling countenance. They were periodically exhorted to buy Roy Acuff flour. ("It ain't genuine if it don't have Roy's picture on it.") In response to their ecstatic shouts ("Sing it purty, Roy!") Roy and his talented crew, in full folk-singer regalia, rewarded them with renditions of "The Wabash Cannon-Ball" and my own favorite, "I'm Walking the Floor Over You." ("I cain't sleep a wink, that is true!") This was all quite remote from the baroque commercial excesses of today's Opryland!

Max Brauer, the Social-Democratic former mayor of Altona, a suburb of Hamburg, was an occasional lecturer. He was an intense florid-faced middle-aged man with no trace of charm. Julius Schwarz, a fellow-soldier who hailed from Hamburg, told me that Brauer would be the city's postwar mayor. I thought this fanciful. But the British installed him in that office after the Allied victory.

November 7, 1943: You may have been reading in the papers about the case of the Penore girl who kidnapped a little 4-year old boy and brought him here to Vanderbilt to try to convince her ex-husband, Gus Tilove, that he was the father. Tilove is one of our FA and L [Foreign Area and Language] boys here, and he has been away for a whole month testifying at her trial.

Gus Tilove was handsome and wiry, his manner weary and ironic. His wife had come to join him in Nashville—a most unusual situation for an enlisted man. But he had to spend his nights in the dormitory. Although he was a staunch anti-Communist, the army placed him under suspicion as a "red." After the war, as Gus Tyler, he became a leading intellectual figure in the American Federation of Labor.

One night, as conversation in our dormitory continued after lights out, a loud voice called out for quiet, and the answer came back: "Fuck you!" The lights went back on and the lieutenant who had demanded silence asked who had said that to him. There was no response, and company punishment was imposed until the perpetrator owned up or was denounced by his peers. The punishment took the form of an arduous series of push-ups and confinement to the dormitory after our normal routine. This continued for several days and elicited considerable grumbling. The evildoer finally acknowledged his guilt (he didn't know, after all, that it was an officer who had told us to shut up), but the interesting part of the story is that he was regarded as a hero for making this confession, rather than as the villain who had caused us several days of discomfort by his refusal to speak up.

An article I wrote, entitled "Soldier Thinking" and signed "G.I.," appeared in *The New Republic*.[2] It suggested that the troops be taught more about the causes and aims of the war.

August, 1943: It's very important that you mention this article to *absolutely no one*. It can mean trouble for me if such information gets around.

Last Sunday afternoon we walked out to the swanky residential suburb of Nashville—Belle Meade. There are some very lovely old estates there. Such a contrast to the monstrous miles of Negro shacks in town. The colored people here are so ill-treated. If one goes into a store to buy something he may wait for an hour before he gets waited on—since white customers are waited on first regardless of when they came in. No wonder there are disorders like the Harlem riots the other day!

August 25, 1943: Dreyfus [identified in chapter 10] came in drunk the other night, having won a beer-drinking contest between 9:30 and 10:30 in the joint across the street. He sang loudly in French and Alsatian but his drunkenness was shown to be a hoax by his failure to urinate.

In Nashville at night, silent and asleep, melancholy train whistles evoked echoes of the blues. By day, the Louisville and Nashville Railroad station, a fortress of gray granite, was thronged with civilians costumed to fit every possible social level and servicemen with suitcases and duffel bags. Here I saw for the first time a German soldier, the back of his green-gray uniform stenciled with a large "PW" (Prisoner of War). He was escorted by two military policemen and appeared bewildered by the sights.

The trains, homes, and industries of Nashville were fueled by bituminous coal. As cool weather came on, the smoke fused with the fogs that rose from the Cumberland River to form a dense smog that sat heavy on our lungs. When we choked on it and coughed, our phlegm was black.

October 31, 1943: My NY furlough was good, though short and sandwiched by odious rail journeys. . . . Milton Klonsky [yet another poet friend from college days] has been married to his Rhoda for five months, though they don't live together and he hasn't told his parents.[3] He is by now a full-fledged neurotic, as he told me very proudly. In fact he had himself discharged from the Army under Section 8 [psychiatric disability] before he was ever put into uniform. (He had been in the Enlisted Reserve Corps). He expected to get a fine job with some war relief agency writing copy, although he is defeatist and cynical. Meanwhile he lives off his parents, sleeps late, and reads poetry. Too bad about our friend Milton.

Balet [the art historian] has been ill. The last eight months have aged and weakened him. I went to hear him lecture and was as impressed and astounded as though I had never heard him before. With all his tremendous force and vitality he hurled himself at the minds before him, made his subject (early Christian art) alive and meaningful. He's a great man. The enormous significance of his work grows on me more and more. *The Twelfth Century* will be one of the major works of scholarship of this century. [This book was never published. It traced the origins of modernity and secularism to the birth of Gothic architecture.] Yet Balet is too worn out and disgusted by the apathy with which all his productive efforts have been met here [in the United States] to finish his book or to work on any new problems. I spent a good deal of my time with him trying to make him realize the importance of his work. Physically he looks the same, as does Mrs. B. We drank the usual tea and ate the usual Dutch fruit cake (no more cigarettes now!) But there's no psychological ease.

Now there's a kind of artificial, inchoate conflict with [the English architect Serge] Chermayeff [later to be the director of the Yale School of Architecture], whose small thoughtless actions and slights are being seized upon as evidence for elaborate theses of antagonism. It's very interesting and sad to see this develop. [Balet had been Chermayeff's sponsor for his teaching job at Brooklyn College after he and his family immigrated to New York at the start of the war.] For Chermayeff too has changed, or perhaps my perspective has altered. It's still the warm bright apartment with the gaudy abstractions on the walls, the highballs lavishly bedecking the round functional wooden table, Mrs. C. functional and beautiful, reclining gracefully on the functional couch, Serge's functional green bust scowling thoughtfully behind the real Serge who gestures with benign expansiveness. Oscar [Brand, my old friend, folk singer and musicologist] had said that there was something unreal and untrue about the Chermayeffs. No, I could see nothing to put my finger on, except an obvious guilt complex with relation to Balet. Maybe there's nothing there that can't be simply explained by the stay-at-home intellectual's frustrations with regard to the war.

When I was home it seemed as though I had been away for only a weekend. Now that I'm back here I don't have the feeling that my city is separated from me by some metaphysical supervoid, as I did during my early weeks at Camp Crowder. In Nashville I feel myself solidly placed in the soil of the American continent. Beyond a certain number of visible tangible valleys and hills and railroad tunnels lies my city, which is also rooted in the firm stable flesh of the extensive earth; there's no gap. One week at home made me realize that I'll never come back there to live. I've left my dear family for good. I'm in the world now.

I have no hopes for a commission; in fact I'm worried about all this training going to waste completely (as it did in the case of the guy who was already sent out of here to the troops and overseas for being a red—orders from Washington). The existence of a G-2 [military intelligence] spy organization here has begun to assume more than shadowy evidence. The people chosen for this kind of assignment, determining the existence of subversive elements, are Coughlinites, Christian Fronters, pro-Fascists. Antisemitism here is on the increase.

Chapter 4

Preparing to Go Over There

The prevailing assumption behind our program of language and area studies was that we were being readied for duty in the military government of a liberated Europe. At one time this may have been the intention, but the army had changed its mind. We were slated for intelligence duties.

January 10, 1944: The classification I was given on the shipping order was as vocal interceptor, which means my job will be to listen to German broadcasts. I am not very enthusiastic about the idea.

Although I had been studying French at Vanderbilt, I was shipped out along with those in the German program, and the emigrés from Germany and Austria. These men had been in the country for only a few years, but they did not cluster into cliques apart from the rest of us. I never heard them speak anything but English to each other.

On the way south, our train stopped to take on coal or water at a small station in Georgia. A small elderly black man was hawking watermelons. A soldier called out, "Sir!" to get his attention. Another commented, "That's the first time in his life he's been called that by a white man."

The army itself was strictly segregated into Negro and Caucasian units, except for the Nisei battalions who fought in Italy and a number of units from Puerto Rico. (I had been pleased and surprised to see that a Nisei sergeant was in charge of a white troop formation at Camp Crowder.) Hispanics were not a significant element in the America of that day. A very dark-skinned man in one of the units in which I served in the South went out of his way to identify himself: "I'm no nigger. I'm a Cuban."

At MacDill Field, in Tampa, the Vanderbilt group was melded with those from ASTP units at other universities. Among these were two men gifted with an extraordinary facility for goofing off. They had adjacent cots on which they managed to spend much of their time languidly reclining while they exchanged information and views on a variety of intellectually rarefied literary topics. One of them, Pfc. Rudy Globus, claimed to have an allergy to detergents that made it medically impossible for him to perform KP. He was exempt while his claim was investigated; since the bureaucratic mills ground slowly, he may well have enjoyed this privilege for the rest of the war. The other litterateur was Donald Maher, a fey, reedy poet with an angry look who led a brief troubled life as an instructor at Columbia University after the war.

January 21, 1944: There are 20 of us from Vanderbilt, all German students, attached to this unit. During the next week we will receive medical exams and be checked by the FBI for work of military secrecy—what we won't know for some time. In the meantime, I'm in the Signal Corps again, attached to Air Corps.

Vint Hill Farms

Having been vetted for top-secret assignments (with a few exceptions among the most compromised former political activists), we were sent back North to the rolling horse country of Virginia, for training in Signal Intelligence at an installation called Vint Hill Farms.

February 2, 1944: This little camp is way out in the woods, forty miles from Washington, and everything that happens here is very secret indeed. "This place doesn't exist," we were told in the latrine. Therefore never never tell anyone exactly where I am or what I do or what kind of a camp it is beyond that it's in the Signal Corps. I still don't know anything about it.

Our mentor was a hard-faced Master Sergeant Middeldorf, who instructed us on the Wehrmacht's battle order and insignia of rank.[1] The bulk of our time was devoted to instruction in cryptanalysis, for which we used self-teaching exercise manuals. The problems became progressively more difficult, and I found them so fascinating that I returned to the classroom to work on them after hours.

The bus went back and forth infrequently. The location was within hitchhiking range of Washington, though travel was not always simple. On one occasion I accepted a rather bumpy ride, in the fetal position, in a car's closed trunk.

February, 1944: My Washington evening was spent at Louise Rosenblatt's [my former English professor]. She is now *the* expert on the French Committee for National Liberation at the FCC Monitoring Service.[2] She claims to know all the news before anyone else and she seems to have qualms about the petty bourgeois conservative aspect of the French Committee. Her husband, [the historian Sidney] Ratner, is with the Post-War Rehabilitation branch of the F.E.A. Funny, you settle down in a living room for a few hours, drink good coffee and wine with people who work with the war in a nice refined intellectual bureaucratic way, and your own contact with things G.I. becomes attenuated to the mere wisp of a thread—until one stands on the bus line and is whisked to the cold barracks of Vint Hill.

On another visit I saw Godzevsky. He had been joined by his wife, a subdued, sad, willowy lady. He must have been highly regarded by his superiors to enjoy such a privilege. When I returned to the States from Europe in 1945, I called the Soviet mission in Washington in the hope of contacting him again and spoke to a suspicious-sounding person who wanted to know my business, which I explained freely. "He has gone back," I was told at last. "Is there some address at which I can write to him?" I asked. "It would be better for him if you didn't write," the voice said quietly. Stalin had already begun his postwar persecutions of those exposed to the West.

I also had the opportunity to make several weekend trips home and to catch up on gossip.

March, 1944: Paul B. [earlier a very Big Man on Campus, later a specialist in public health], married and an actual or expectant father, dreaded the thought of going into the Army so much (I can just see the tears well in the poor boy's eyes at the thought) that he developed stomach ulcers and made 4-F. As a result he has been expelled from his extra-curricular [Young Communist League] activities as a "slacker" and goes around with a politically dazed expression on his face.

New York gave me a sensation on my brief visits that I never had when I was on furlough. The Times Square crowd of bar-spangled officers and their perfumed wenches reminds me nauseatingly and frighteningly of Thackeray's "Vanity Fair." Despite all the uniforms, there is no contact between the city and the war that goes on and on every day, killing men and destroying cities. I feel ill at ease in NY. All of my past seems a series of aimless visions now, unrelated to anything the present means or the future hopes for. Where shall we all strike root, I wonder. Millions and millions of us, our discharge papers in our pockets, walking the streets in search of work, of security, of a political faith that is practical and yields results.

Order posted on the bulletin board of another unit:

Subject: Defecation in buildings
To: All members this command
1. Certain members of this command have been defecating in the basement of the mess hall building. This disgusting habit is contrary to all human and social codes.
2. Such action normally expected only of animals must cease at once.

3. Anyone found guilty of this obnoxious act will be court-martialled to the fullest extent under Articles of War.
4. It is the duty of anyone observing this act to immediately report it. Failure to do so will also be met by court martial under Articles of War.

Captain ———, Commanding

In similar military style, a mimeographed notice appeared on bulletin boards each day reading something like this: "The Sun will rise today at 0623 hours and set at 1844 hours. By order of Major General ———."

The course in cryptanalysis ended, and we returned to MacDill Field.

March 29, 1944: We were shipped back here at the end of last week on a few hours' notice, just in time to evade our longed-for weekend pass. The trip, by Southern Railroad day coaches, of course, took 48 hours instead of the required 24, because some fuck-up of a transportation officer had bought tickets on the wrong railroad. Immediately on arrival I was assigned to seven days of KP, although I had done 7 days just before I was sent on D.S. [Detached Service]. (I was removed after the second day to attend a training course.) The company commander informed the boys that ratings would be few and would come only after a long time. What I have seen of the officers makes me frightened to realize that these men will be in charge of my life in battle, and that they are in direction of as important an organization as this. The C.O. [commanding officer], who maintains a 1st sgt. with an established IQ of 88, is much more interested in the parade appearance than in the combat efficiency of the unit. For instance, it is considered more important for us to weed the scraggly sandy lawn than to have review classes in our language work.

There were occasional reminders of battles in Brooklyn that seemed as venomous as those on the global scene:

April 10, 1944: From Balet's letter it sounded as though the attack [on him within the faculty] had taken the dangerous turn of alien-baiting and a revival of canards along the lines of "I wouldn't go fishing with B. He is so brutish! And anti-religious too, as exemplified by [his reference to] the statement of [the surrealist poet] André Breton: 'God is a piece of chewing gum.'"

My time on "duty" has been divided between weed-pulling, completely haphazard, disorganized and worthless military training and just plain fucking off. I don't suppose my state of disillusionment can in any way compare with that of the ASTPs who are now riflemen in infantry outfits, but it is demoralizing to feel the days of "war" slip by and to know yourself far less of a participant than you were 15 months before.[3] Typical of the use of manpower in this outfit is the case of the cook's assistant, who has a cryptographer's spec [military specialty] number. Typical of the officer personnel is the lieutenant who, when saluted by a strange soldier on a street not even in the company area, orders the soldier to police up some papers lying on the sidewalk. ["Policing" was the military term for picking up litter, which usually consisted of cigarette butts.]

Tampa's waterfront is mostly empty lots; the slums are monotonous and devoid of the fervid stir of humanity that usually animates crowded areas. At the greyhound racing track a gay assemblage in evening gowns and Palm Beach clothes repairs nightly to watch the skillful exhibition of the gallant, aristocratic beasts, whose high-spirited dolichocephalic dignity represents the essence of the white supremacy for which our boys are fighting. As one munches one's 20 cent frankfurter [an outrageously high price, compared with the 10 cent hot dogs at Nathan's in Coney Island.] and sips one's 25 cent beer, as one admires the sophisticated banter of the distinguished audience and the fine blue uniforms of the men who parade the dogs before the grandstand and place them in their proper kennels, one's heart swells with a great pride in the accomplishments—present and future—of this great sovereign state of Florida. No amount of revolutionary change can possibly have value and significance unless due reverence is paid to such institutions as this, which carry men's precious heritage.

MacDill Field is located on an island in the middle of Tampa Bay. On Sunday, an old ferryboat transported us around the peninsula of St. Petersburg and up the Gulf Coast to Clearwater Beach. The sun sparkled on aquamarine waters and pristine white sand beaches. The only building that loomed over the treetop line was the pink Don CeSar Hotel, converted into a rehabilitation center for wounded airmen. When I hitchhiked to the center of St. Pete the road went through miles of wasteland, on which ambitious land developers in the 1920's had set signs designating 231st Street, 232nd Street, and so on, though the city's inhabited areas did not go beyond two digits.

April 18, 1944: I sit before our open-air bandshell awaiting commencement of the evening's "Gay 90s" melodrama, performed by the public-spirited folk of Tampa's Little Theater group. In the background already hover some of the characters—17-year-old undraftables with patently phony handlebar mustaches. The loudspeakers regale us with a potpourri overture consisting of "Oh What a Beautiful Morning," "Dixie," "Loch Lomond" and "Old Man River."

The cultural activities of MacDill Field center in the small room on the second floor of the Service Club, where the literati gather nightly to hear the word of Cpl. Zimmermann, bearer of a red nose, which marks him either as a violent drinker or a fanatic sunbather, and of a polished effeminate speech pattern indicative of past history as a college tutor or high school English teacher. Cpl. Z. believes that all art is a history of struggle between classic and romantic strains, and that Gershwin should be played only in whorehouses.

Now it's morning in the barracks: noise and chatter, Giants and Dodgers. "Fuckin' North Dakota hill-billies!" says Brenner of Steinke. "They never saw a baseball bat till they came to the fuckin' movies." "Out there we use baseball bats for toothpicks!" retorts Steinke. "C'mere Steinke," interjects little Abie Rosenblum. "I got a hard-on."

Thus far our principal activity has been lawn-weeding. Our C.O. delivers little sermons on military discipline, threatening us with 5 days in bed (no reading or writing allowed) or endless work details of a particularly gruesome character: "And your hands—brother, your hands are going to be a sight to behold!"

Unless the president is reelected this fall we may very well be going to war again in another ten years, with Russia probably,—and I can see in very practical terms, as exemplified by the primaries right here in Tampa—how enormously strong the appeasers and do-nothings and dunderheads are. Hell, even a progressive guy like [Senator Claude] Pepper has to come out for "white supremacy" and the "pure white" primary.[4] Typical of the liberal approach to practical politics in these times is a full-page ad paid for by the nickels and dimes of Tampa's trade unionists, published by their Labor Council. It attacks a candidate for the state Attorney Generalship whose campaign has been based on the most vicious attacks against labor, and concludes with the lame statement, "But you don't have to vote for this guy! Here are two other candidates who haven't made anti-labor statements."

Florida was at this point in the midst of a primary election campaign, whose outcome was decisive in those days of the Solid (Democratic) South. I went to hear the great liberal, Senator Pepper, defend himself at a street-corner rally. His opponent's chief weapon was a newspaper clipping that showed Pepper shaking hands with a black minister outside a church where the Senator had delivered a guest sermon. Since blacks were *de facto* denied the ballot, Pepper was evidently not courting their vote, but his mere appearance among them was enough to arouse the bile of the die-hard segregationists. To his red-neck audience, he explained that he had "told those niggers how lucky they were to be living in this country, and how they should know their place. And when this nigger preacher put out his hand, naturally I had to shake it."

Tuesday, D-Day, June 6, 1944: I am alerted for what will almost certainly be an overseas shipment. I can't tell you how happy this news makes me.

All day long, sitting in the barracks and listening to the invasion news, I had the most uncomfortable feeling that while the greatest events of our lifetime were taking place 3000 miles away I am doing almost nothing. The sooner I and a lot of other boys go over to do our jobs the sooner the war will be finished.

Another furlough brought me back to New York.

June 20, 1944: One evening I went to see "Decision" and became involved in a theater party, which featured 60 Brooklyn College co-eds in all their perfumed painted finery. They explain how "Decision" (a perfectly dandy straightforward unpretentious antifascist play) is undialectical and un-Aristotelian and how confused the author is and how soldiers never read newspapers or kept up with current events, but how the AYD [American Youth for Democracy, a Communist front] and the Sweethearts of Servicemen [yet another] were helping to show them the light. Silly horrid nasty little girls.

Klonsky is a shipfitter's helper at 60 per and wears an impressive composition helmet. He reports the utter degeneracy of Chester Kallman, who works for the Censorship in NY and has had his overcoat, clock, radio and typewriter stolen by the sailors he brings home at night.

June 20, 1944: For the first time in my life I have found myself marshalling all my powers of sophistry in defense of the Pope of Rome. I was waiting for the bus and found myself in conversation with someone who commenced with several lamentations of a very general character regarding the misfortunes of war. (He was trying to get a candy-stand concession in the park and somehow connected his lack of success with the military situation.) "Tell me," he demanded insidiously. "What are you fighting for?" In a few terse oversimplifications I told him. His opinion was that the war was nothing more than the product of papal intrigue. It thus became my unfortunate duty to recite to the poor man a lecture on the holiness and purity of the Catholic Church and the necessity for unity among Americans of all faiths in this historically critical time.

My final training before going overseas took place at a toughening-up camp at Greensboro, North Carolina, where I was ordered to shimmy along what seemed like a block-long pole extended over a trench twenty feet deep. I froze early in the passage, but the army sent me overseas anyway, despite this evidence of my patent unfitness for the rigors of war.

Chapter 5

The Theater of War

On July 25, the Allied armies broke through the German lines that had contained them in Normandy and began their sweep to Paris (which fell on August 25) and on to the prewar border with Germany.[1] During these critical months, I was well on my way to the war, but not yet in the thick of it. First there was a series of stops in Great Britain.

We embarked on the *Queen Mary* from the West Side docks of Manhattan. I had overloaded my duffel bag with books and other personal paraphernalia and lugged it with great difficulty in the endless files of boarding troops. The great liner had been refitted as a troop ship, but her interior still carried decorative traces of her former luxury.

The Crossing

July, 1944: Letter of unmentionable date, written standing (like too many of my letters), only this one begins to the tune of loud cheerful operatic schmaltz music being played from a recording over the amplifying network of the transport, and the shouts and catcalls of soldiers behind my back, and the vague hum and vibration of the ship's motors, engines, propellers and other miscellaneous machinery of conveyance. And far below the rail at my side, the hush and rush of the gentle waves retreating from our plunging path.

The music has disappeared now, giving way to a British news broadcast which I can't make out in the general hubbub. Brief phrases, names react on my ear— "Riga," "Marshal Konev"—. Somewhere, not so very far away as formerly, the real war is proceeding, our future fate is being decided, and I sit on the high seas all ignorant of current history, yearning to sink my eyes into a fresh full morning newspaper. When I go below I shall ask after the news and get a few brief extracts: "Nothing new. The Russians took some more towns; I can't remember the names." So I know, in only a half-knowing sort of way, unsubstantiated by solid newsprint, that Lublin has fallen (Lublin, the great Nazi slaughterhouse for Jews!) in a victory bigger than Stalingrad, and Warsaw is being neared, and that the heads of German officers are rolling. But this is, as I said, not a real knowl-

The RMS *Queen Mary*. Courtesy Cunard Line.

edge. I must get ashore, read back numbers of the press, and reestablish myself as my own contemporary.

After all, an infantryman in the thick of any crucial battle, his attentions fully occupied with his own small particular mission involving one shed or one acre, goes for days or weeks or more without any sense of the aggregate of battles, of the war as a whole.

My reports on several entertaining days cannot be delivered chronologically, because events on board this big boat resolve themselves into cycles rather than sequence. To begin with, I am impressed with the natural and carefree way in which everyone reacts since the beginning of the journey and deduce from this continued normalcy a primary law of humanity, applicable to all situations of crisis. We are traveling on an angry and dangerous errand. Of the smiling legions chattering, smoking, chewing Hershey bars or reading comic books at every hand, a goodly number are traveling to death, insanity or corporeal affliction. Yet there is a great security in the inevitable G.I. regimentation, and with sufficient imagination, or rather, lack of any, this all becomes just another troop movement—rather long and strange, to be sure—but proceeding according to the rules, under the sheltering aegis of the genial G.I. god.

I sniff the cold salt wet air voraciously, searching the changing, swelling texture of the water, seeing its color change from gray to slate to the purest navy blue spotted with foam bubbling and spraying a fairy intricacy of pattern on the surface. And standing on some high deck, noting the precise constant curvature of the horizon, we shall authoritatively and finally establish the truth of Galileo's theory that the earth is round.

Does it strike you as strange to learn that I stand on the deck of this boat, writing a letter, regarding the waves break into swishing foam off the side, inhaling the spray and blowing my nose as a somewhat free man, untrammeled by grave restrictions? It surprises me too. I marvel to think of it. I keep out of my quarters except when the urgent exigencies of natural or military function demand my presence there. (They are very noisy and uncomfortable. The floor is always crowded with non-intellectual people playing cards for large sums of money, coughing as though in the last stages of galloping consumption, and calling each other, without affection, "damnyankee," "rebel bastard," and numerous sexual names.)

Most of the time I do what I will, within the narrow circle of possibility, which is quite unlike my former fears and fancies of endless discipline and chickenshit. My own main form of entertainment, aside from talking and looking about me, is reading. I read, in the nautical mood, Jack London's "Cruise of the Snark," then Arnold Bennett's "Buried Alive," and Mark Twain's "Life on the Mississippi." Put down after a while, because it bored me, Joseph Conrad's "Mirror of the Sea." All these in small pocket G.I. editions for the use of troops overseas.

There are two forms of official, planned entertainment for us: one, the religious services which are held every day in an almost continuous performance; and two, the movies, which are presented by day on the crowded, cold, damp deck, and at night in the crowded, hot, damp dining room. The first night that the ubiquitous nagging loudspeakers announced a movie, I was already as snugly ensconced as it is possible to be snugly ensconced in a cot on a troopship. But I got up eagerly, dressed and hurried down, down, down to the mess hall, which was packed and smelled bad from too many people. Dauntlessly and intrepidly I fought my way through the crowd and found a spot on a bench in the very middle of the hall. The lights went out, the audience oohed and whistled expectantly as preliminary messages lit up the screen—and then there was a gasp of disappointment as the title of the film hove into view. The chaplains—intriguing unscrupulous clerics that they are, had provided us with religious movies. Embedded as I was in the middle of the crowd, I was helpless, unable to flee until the conclusion of the first picture.

This same mess hall, whose luxurious appointments recall the time when it was a "dining room" in the best of style, is twice daily the scene of one of our principal ordeals—eating. The process of preparing to eat, eating and rehabilitat-

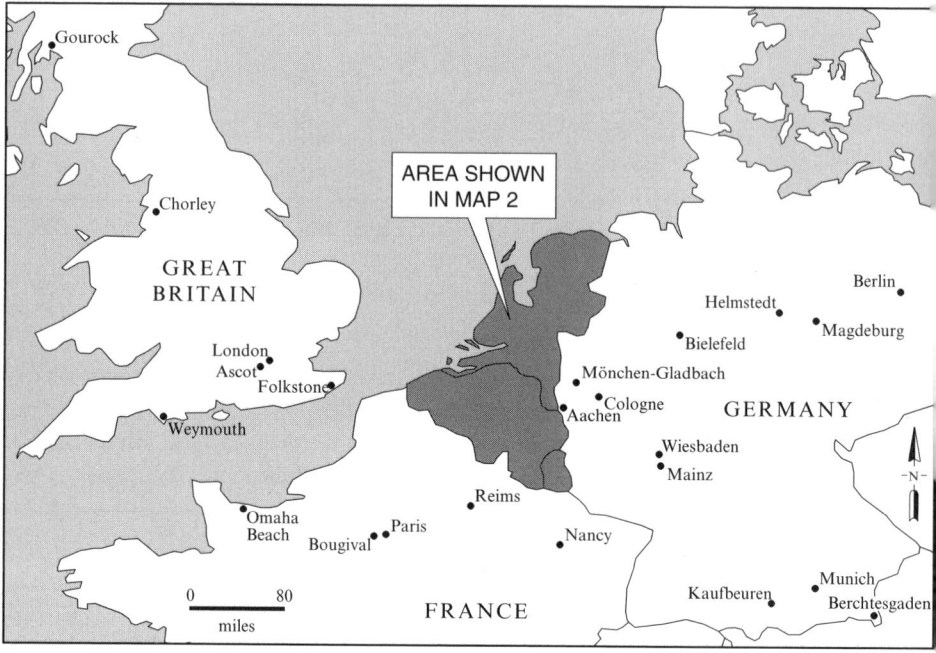

Map 1. Western Europe.

ing myself afterwards takes only one hour altogether, but it is the most fearful, frenzied hasty hour man can create or spend. The business of feeding us is managed with an impersonal efficiency that I can compare to the human circulatory system.

The mess hall, throbbing with energy in the bowels of the ship, is like a great heart. The capillary trickle of prospective diners issues from various quarters, merges in corridors and at stairheads into venous currents that finally pour into the heart in a huge powerful steady stream. Then out of the mess hall again in a sluggish current—the mess-kit washing line—and back through the labyrinthine ways that lead to temporary home. And at every step of the way that leads into the heart and back again there is some minor authority to crack the whip and urge you along at greater speed: "On the double!" "Hurry up!" "C'mon, let's go!" While you gobble your food with marathon haste, the sad KPs urge you on to finish quickly, quit stalling, stop eating so much. And at the mess-kit washing post you only have time to get your greasy hardware slightly wet before mysterious forces hustle you into another line. The various lines, incidentally, are of a very long and complicated nature. People have been known to go through the same queue a number of times and never get fed or get their kits cleaned at all!

Eating was our second worst ordeal. The least pleasant by far are our postpon-

Map 2. Benelux: Belgium, the Netherlands, and Luxembourg.

able but hardly avoidable trips to the latrine. We perform all our functions on the wide or duty ends of siphon-like bowls, whose outer rims are padded with toilet paper, when there is any, in a feeble attempt at sanitation. The American soldier is the most self-consciously sanitary soldier in the world.

The *Queen* moved faster than any submarine, so she crossed the Atlantic without a destroyer escort. One day, fortunately when I was on deck, there was a submarine scare. Klaxons sounded, the engines went full throttle, and the mighty ship executed a sudden and remarkable ninety-degree turn.

One interesting thing about this ship. For reasons of obvious impracticability there is no segregation of Negro troops—except insofar as they are quartered together in their Jim Crow units. Unfortunately a lot of these boys let loose with unbridled passions on the food in the mess hall, where the boarding house, or catch-as-catch-can, method of self-service is employed. It's more than just the bad manners one has every right to expect; eating plays a definite part in the pattern of compensation—an old story. (Pretty clear, isn't it, that our Army's Jim Crow policy simply encourages this sort of thing, provides no genteel yardsticks or leavening agents.) White and Negro soldiers don't appear to be mixing socially, though, while British soldiers mix with colored (they call them "African") troops almost as readily as with us. There have been no racial clashes that I know of; everyone's in pretty good humor.

    It's easy to look back on now—but getting on to this boat was unquestionably the most arduous job any of us has yet performed in the Army. Always before, when we moved, there were convenient trucks and trains to move our heavy permanent gear out of the way. But on this trip our poor bodies carried all the burden, which was all arranged in a thousand unmanageable bundles, whose aggregate weight fell cruelly in awkward tender places. The damned gun I had slung on my shoulder kept sliding off and threatening murder to the innocent fellow behind me. And to add insult to injury, the usual silly happy band was always jauntily oompahing away at crucial moments and expecting my faltering feet to keep in step with its arbitrary drum beats.

    On the pier, in a brief breathing-space, I discovered where your Red Cross pennies go. They go for limeade, delicious thirst-quenching, energy-rich, life-giving limeade, which you drink standing in ranks, swallowing great hunks of sugared doughnut the while. (It's all a studied part of the embarking process. I never would have gotten aboard on my own steam without that cup of limeade as fuel at just the point when it was administered. Everything was the acme of efficiency in an utterly fantastic way, of which I would never have dreamed the Army capable.) Your Red Cross pennies also go for a little kit that every soldier gets on board—containing sewing equipment, pencil, paper, playing cards, a pack of cigarettes, gum drops, shoe laces, razor blades, soap and one Pocket Book (paper back). In addition, each of us received a carton of cigarettes (I gave mine away, pure that I am) donated by various CIO local unions (mine was a smelter workers' local in Oklahoma. It made me kind of guilty thinking of the poor smelter workers, when, after all, what have we done to deserve all this? And I was angry too, at the smelter workers for buying cigarettes, and leading young unspoiled soldier lads into the foul ways of tobacco. No kidding).

I spoke to some German-speaking soldiers who have had frequent contact with Nazi prisoners of war for quite a while. They had encouraging things to say; there has been a decline in belligerence and pro-Nazi feeling; in fact they used the word "docile" to describe the latest specimens. But they report no change in the fanatical personal loyalty of the Germans to Hitler himself. The Gestapo and Party are blamed for the failures, rather than the Führer. I asked what proportion of the German soldiers are salvageable as human beings; they feel that the vast majority can be reeducated. They had found no evidence of anti-Semitism among the Germans, which brings to mind Dr. Brauer's (the fat burgomaster of Altona) remark [in one of his lectures to us at Vanderbilt] that after the war Germany would have less anti-Semitism than any country in the world, and our own sardonic comment that there could hardly be any anti-Semitism after you had butchered the last Jew. But apparently the average German soldier is unaware of the horrible policy of extermination being carried out in the east of Europe by the SS and the Gestapo.

It's next morning now. Fleecy masses of cotton-gray clouds are scurrying across the skies at a level so low that I feel as though I could reach up and touch them if I climbed the mast. And the sun shining through the open spaces has gilded a great sector of the water so that now it's all glimmering gold and silver. On the distant horizon a miracle has taken form. Dim blue silhouette of proud craggy summits rising sharply from the sea. Tiny miniature promise of the earth, shadow of Europe—Ireland, not emerald yet, purple-gray outpost, ringed by rocks like a fortress with battlements. The first seagulls are winging about our stern. It is rumored that one stayed with the ship all the way from America, but I haven't seen it myself.

The hillbillies in our cabin last night made a racket till 1:00 A.M. They reproached each other for eating at the same table with niggers, Jews and the like. Altman, who sleeps above me, was regaled with gin whiskey by some drunken officers (if an enlisted man were caught with liquor on the boat he'd have the book thrown at him) and threatened to be seasick all over me and the other guys beneath.

At our last camp in the States, the Italian prisoners are now organized in labor battalions, and have the freedom of the post, which they cannot leave. Some of them were assigned as permanent KPs in our mess hall. Except for sex, the long absence of which they bemoan bitterly, they appear to be having the time of their life. The Italian-speaking guys among us carried on brisk conversations with them. A cheery, *"É, paesano!"* was good for a double helping every time. And the day that spaghetti was served—ah, an orgy! The Italians, incidentally, were much more robust-looking specimens than I had expected.

Now we can see the shore clearly. Green lawn, black cliff, patches of field. Except for a lighthouse no sign of life ashore. Every man a Columbus in sentiment.

The water near shore changes color, becomes a rich green-black. Now I understand why the Gulf at Florida was such pure bright aquamarine.

Later [Gourock, Scotland, near Glasgow]: I am now sunning myself in a British harbor. Harry Y. is leaning over the rail at my side and cautions me to be indefinite for security reasons and say "Somewhere in a British harbor." We are waiting to debark and our eyes rove happily over the landscape, which is clean and green and covered with gingerbread houses. (I don't think the Censor would like me to say any more, would you Censor? He says no, the nasty little brute.) One of the boys said to me that he was surprised to feel so completely at home in a strange country so far from home. I too feel this; I'm not conscious of anything unnatural about the scenery or my own place in it. Any situation becomes immediately normal when it is transmuted from its notion into objective fact.

July 30, 1944: The ocean crossing had many uncomfortable aspects, of course, but I enjoyed it enormously nonetheless. I had never before realized how deeply blue sea water is.

Chorley

As the result of what was now to us a familiar military blunder, we were sent, not to a reception center for arriving troops, but to an air base near Chorley, a dreary mill town in Lancashire. From there, airmen who had completed their thirty-mission bombing tours were being processed for return to the States. A good proportion of them appeared to have been unbalanced by their stressful experiences. One lieutenant walked about giving highly convincing imitations of enemy anti-aircraft fire. His arms swept through the air as he recalled the thud of the explosions around him: "Rrrooom! Rrrooom! Rrrooom!" Such encounters offered slim reassurance as we awaited our own fate.

July, 1944: I'm now at a camp "in England," washed, shaved, very well fed and occupying the upper half of the bed that fills most of the cubicle room I share with Harry. It's got a window opened wide on a lush green meadow, stunted oak trees and the red roofs of houses in the background. Everything is perfectly groomed, cultivated, cherished. Flower gardens everywhere, wherever there's a free square foot of soil.

Our official welcome to the British Isles was delivered at the blacked-out station of a little town at which the train stopped for a few minutes. On the platform stood a reception committee of one, his cheeks cheery though hollow with approaching old age, a checked cap jauntily set on his head, a faint but unmistakable scent to his breath. Fortune sent him to our window. "Yanks, is it?" he cried, shook a dozen hands mightily, and brought forth a huge bottle of tasty ale and a small gill bottle of Scotch whiskey, whose contents we quickly consumed. We presented him with cigarettes and chewing gum and serenaded him with "Should old acquaintance be forgot?" [He also warned us, through a formidable burr, to beware of the race of foul blackguards we were about to encounter on the other side of the Scottish border.] The train started to move; these British trains start smooth as velvet. The old-timer shook more hands and raised his paw in farewell as we pulled away. "Shove it up 'is bloody arse!" he roared.

A casual street conversation led to an invitation to speak about America to the members of a working-class discussion club. Although Chorley was full of G.I.s, these people had apparently never talked to any of them. They listened to me with the same curiosity that might have greeted a visitor from Ubangi or Tannu Tuva. Close to Chorley was the town of Wigan, a standing butt of British music hall jokes about its non-existent pier.[2] A local told me, "We do have a peer, and a very good one, Lord—[the name didn't register]!"

Chorley, August 4, 1944: I was in an old manor house the other evening that had been built in the fifteenth century, before the discovery of America. Everywhere one sees flower gardens and marvelous smooth green lawns. It has been possible for me to enjoy my evenings fully despite the blackout, for with double daylight saving time it doesn't get dark until ll o'clock at night. The British don't rent their bikes; they're a necessity, with transportation as short as it is, and it's almost impossible to find one. I found a fellow who lent me his; he refused to accept money, but took the American cigarettes I had gotten from the Red Cross on the boat. His brother-in-law and sister had me in for tea and cookies when I returned the other night.

One of our boys had saved an orange and gave it to a little kid. I don't think he had ever tasted an orange before. He ran away to show the prize to his friends and they all came back with him admiringly.

I came to a bridge across a small river and found the air filled with a ceaseless tolling of chimes, which appeared to come from all directions but actually came from a small church on a hillside. A little old workingman told me that the chimes were run by relays of men who practiced on them in a long tradition. In this same town I saw a whole family riding one bicycle: mama and papa each at a set of pedals and baby trundling along beside in an outcarriage. And I also saw for the first time U.S. Negro soldiers in the company of white women, who were obviously prostitutes. From what I can gather, despite all the stories, Negro soldiers are *not* accepted by English girls with the same avidity that awaits their white compatriots.

This same evening, too, I was a spectator at a scene that is vivid in my memory. It was late in the evening, twilight time; outside a fish-and-chips establishment off the main square, a crowd had gathered around a girl and a woman in an argument. The crowd was civilian—kids, whores, workers and their wives, miscellaneous slum folk—and a British sailor or two, some soldiers, British and American, white and black. The woman, middle-aged, was nagging and screaming at the girl, a prostitute, pretty, slender, tall and well, refinedly, made up.

I don't know whether there was specific cause for the older woman's anger or whether it was just the general prevalence of sin in the locality. But the girl kept her head high and her eyes and tongue flashing. "I works for me livin'! I works for me livin'! Don't you call me a Piccadilly girl. I wish I were a Piccadilly girl! They get five pounds a night, they do! I works for me livin'!" The older woman kept up her nagging. She tugged at the dark blue jacket the whore wore over her shoulders. The girl snapped out, suddenly fierce. "You lay your fingers off that coat, you hear? That's me husband's coat!" The other cackled cynically, "Hah—your husband!" "Yes, the girl said proudly, "My husband. My husband what was killed in the war two years ago."

The tensions that had held the scene together suddenly disappeared. The crowd disintegrated. The fish-and-chip shop became amazingly full in a twinkling. One of the colored boys dropped his newspaperful of soggy potato chips in the gutter. He guffawed loudly, and his powdered little blonde whore tugged angrily at his arm. For a brief moment, a brief hour, the world seems a wild surrealist kaleidoscope of mad passions, living deaths cavorting on the English cobblestones, ghouls and ghosts and crazy dream creatures cavorting in a masquerade, the Night Town episode of *Ulysses*. The people who paraded the darkening streets seemed ill, malformed, broken or twisted, some strange casual compound oozing from a crack in the cauldron. The impression only strengthened as I waited for the train in the blacked-out railroad station, with the jet lamp cutting the void from the high ceiling and lighting eerily on the faces of the passersby.

I am impressed by the compact, or rather, congested way in which English industrial towns are laid out. Standing at the top of a hill I could see a whole city nestled in a valley that would just about hold a small American suburb.

My friend and I entered a smoke-filled compartment containing a boy, a British soldier, a worker, and a businessman with the face of an American Southerner. In the corner was a little old man who looked exactly like John D. Rockefeller at the age of 95. His few wisps of hair were pasted flat to his pink skull. Big ears protruded from his bony, paste-white face, on whose drawn, wrinkled skin glowed a scarlet bulb of a nose and thin orange lips framing a set of false teeth. He wore a bright tan tweed sports jacket and a vivid polka-dot tie drawn to the loosest of knots. His white straw hat hung on the rack over his head. He spoke in a thick regional dialect, with highly alcoholic overtones, and he spoke incessantly on any subject he happened to think of.

Various facts emerged: a. he was retired after 45 years in the business; b. the business was beer and hairdressing; c. he was married to his sister—"not for lust"—and his sister was the woman who ran the place now and yelled "Time!" and "Time is time!" at 10 o'clock [the legal closing hour]; d. he was returning from a few days of boozing in the city because his place had had to close its doors; (no more liquor or beer until Friday at 5:30; obviously he couldn't patronize his competitors); e. he was 61 (!) years old but his hand was steady as a rock (he held it out, a cold white skeleton of a hand, but steady as a rock). The place that this miserable drunken corpse owned was the Imperial Hotel, "the Imp," a great furnace of life and heat and vice! Oh, the world is all extremes, a fantastic bundle of fraud and anarchy.

August 8, 1944: It's hard to believe sometimes that the British have been at war for four long years, but the evidence of this is in the living standards and in the attitudes and habits of the people. Wherever an American soldier goes, the kids, ragged and otherwise, tag along for gum and candy. The stick of gum means to them all the little luxuries of childhood that they've missed.

August, 1944: Unobtrusive bar, operated by a most "refoined" barlady. The beer was more expensive and much more tasteful than any I've tasted in England. (It still had the same interesting effect on the kidneys.) On a sofa in the corner an old British naval officer and his young wife were being told very obscene stories by a hysterical drunken dwarf in fancy riding boots and breeches and with a silk scarf tucked into his little tweed jacket.

Speaking of drunks: very charming little episode on the truck going back to camp the other night. A few minutes before deadline—curfew time—a staggering lieutenant led by a prostitute approached the rear of our truck, which was the first in line. He was too far gone to climb up into it under his own power; between her pushing and our pulling he got on and slumped in a heap on the floor, leaning against the tailgate. Every few seconds, regularly, his body was convulsed with an enormous hiccup that threatened to become an eruption.

The truck was just about to start when a huge soldier, not wearing hat or coat, scrambled aboard and sat down on the tailgate, almost on top of the sad lieutenant. The newcomer had also had a little too much. He weaved back and forth as the truck bounced along the road and alternated between loud singing of popular songs and laments over the loss of his blouse which had just been "stolen by some Limey bastard." Suddenly he became aware of the pathetic figure at his feet. He dealt it a resounding fraternal smack. "How ya doing, kid?" There was no response.

The Big Guy started what was apparently a set routine of patter regarding his five years' stay in Roossia during the Revolootion, when the streets ran red with blood and we put people in cement. He sang several songs in his bellowing voice, cursed the thief of his jacket, and solemnly told the lieutenant that six years ago there wasn't a wrestler who could beat him; he had crushed that nigger in St. Louis, and now look at him!

The lieutenant suddenly becomes a human being with eyeglasses and a Southern accent to his dull drunken voice. "Rugged!" he muttered sarcastically. "Rugged!" the big fellow snorted. "You bet it's rugged. Hey, what's your name, lootenint?" "Jones," lied the lieutenant. "Jonesey," the big guy continued, "What outfit you in?" The lootenint became concerned. "Hey, you better not talk to me like that," he said from the floor. The big guy laughed ferociously. "Listen kid, you know who you talkin' to? I'm the MONISTER, see, the MONISTER! Six years ago there wasn't a wrestler in the States who could keep me down. You think I give a shit what any schoolboy tells me? I can take you in my hands and crush you to a pulp. In Russia we crushed 'em in cement. The blood flowed like borshch!" "I know you're bigger'n I am," said the lootenint dully.

The Monister began to holler, *"Bésame, bésame mucho."*[3] Then he began to curse the damn-Limey-bastard-who-had-stolen-his-blouse-but-if-he-expected-to-find-a-wallet-in-it-he-was-out-of-luck. By that time we were in camp already and turned off the road down a side path leading through the woods. Both the Monister and the lootenint awoke to sudden realization that they should have gotten off half a mile back. They shouted and shrieked till the truck stopped. They half-jumped, half-fell out of the truck. I last saw them standing together in the dark forest, leaning against each other and lighting matches to see where they were.

A Critical Decision

From our ranks, a contingent was to be sent on flying duty. Those who drew this assignment were to sit in the lead plane of each bomber formation, listening to Luftwaffe communications, and warning the commanding officer of enemy preparations and tactics.

The criteria for inclusion on this roster were the same as those for other flight personnel, and I lacked the requisite 20/20 vision, like many of the other eye-glassed intellectuals in our group. Since the results fell short of the needed quota, a new call went out for unmarried volunteers who agreed to waive the physical requirements.

That night I walked the streets of Chorley (still sunlit at 10:00 P.M. because of the war's double daylight-savings time) in long and agonized colloquy with my friend, a budding economist named Bob Strotz. He refused to sign up, in spite of vague threats that the recalcitrants would be sent to the infantry. As a student of probability theory, he correctly reasoned that the chances of his demise were considerably greater in the air over Germany than somewhere else on the ground, and he earnestly tried to persuade me that one's own neck was what counted for most. But if everyone felt that way, I argued, nobody would accept dangerous duty and the war would be lost. I had to subordinate myself to the larger objective of saving the world from evil. The next morning I signed the waiver; Strotz did not, and faced no consequences. With the addition of the volunteers, the flying duty roster was filled.

August, 1944: I was supposed to fly with the 8th Air Force over Germany (I passed the physical, signed the waiver, etc.), but by some strange fluke the quota was overfilled, and three names (including mine) were shifted [at random] to the 3rd Radio Squadron Mobile (G).

Of the others who had gone on to flying duty, a high proportion became casualties or were taken prisoner. Among them was a gentle soul whom I had first met in Nashville and who, in retrospect, remarkably resembled the actor Telly Savalas. He was the victim of a disease that, like a radiation treatment for cancer, had eliminated all the hair on his face, head, and body. Undoubtedly he had a proper name, but he was universally known as "Timoshenko," after the shaven-headed Soviet field marshal, and he responded cheerfully to this jibe. To cover his bare pate, Timoshenko wore an incredibly crude and unconvincing wig, the color of milk chocolate, that must have been made of a synthetic fiber. He removed it before showering and at bedtime, and since it was generally covered by his forage cap, there was some speculation as to whether it would adhere to his skull or to the cap when it was removed. Since baldness was not a disqualifying physical disability for flying duty, Timoshenko joined the contingent that went to the 8th Air Force. He was killed when his bomber was shot down.[4]

Ascot

The other non-flying members of our contingent were now sent to a camp near Ascot, west of London and within commuting range of the city. Disconcertingly, in the midst of the war, the races were still on, attended by gentlemen in pearl-gray top hats and ladies in pre-War finery. A few miles away was the bleak proletarian city of Slough, whose numerous pubs enticed the fun-loving among us. Also nearby was Eton, with splendid red brick buildings and little boys in ridiculous straw hats. I gravitated to London at the first opportunity.

August, 1944: Went to Windsor, Eton and the village [Stoke Poges] where Gray wrote his *Elegy*. Tried to get into the British Museum, but it was closed. Most of the museums have evacuated their collections for the duration.

August 27, 1944: Slow bus to the theater, went to the lobby, was directed to the back stairs, double-timed it up four or five stories to the gallery, didn't take change for my ticket and *then* discovered that I had missed the first act not of

"The Marriage of Figaro," which I had run to see, but of "Madame Butterfly," which would have called forth no such haste. The program had been changed. Well, it was quite well done and I came back the next night for more Puccini to see "La Bohème." No startling voices of the sort one hears at the Metropolitan, but not a trace of incompetence either. Sadler's Wells Opera; sets and orchestra very good. I was surprised at the small audience Friday night. It was about half full in the balcony (cheap seats, only 1/6 [one shilling sixpence] or 20 cents) but Saturday the place was packed. "Mme. Butterfly" struck me as a cheap commercial theme, while "La Bohème" seemed much more genuine and appealing. Sung in English, but I couldn't understand the words anyway.

I have a queer idea that tragic opera is all phony. The great early operatic composers, culminating in Mozart, recognized the limitations on reality imposed by the conditions in which musical drama could be performed as a secular amusement. They left tragedy and drama to the realm of religious music—the oratorio—and made their operas down to earth and comic. Then in the middle and late 19th century when the bourgeoisie in its new heights of power and glory demanded a secular tragedy, the new school of tragic opera developed, dignifying the most commonplace trite little individual problems with ponderous performances and heroic music. That is what I, from my 1944 perspective, cannot stomach. The individualist art of the pre–World War I era dealt in family conflicts. Our social era is absorbed with the problems of man in the mass.

I had the same feeling yesterday when I visited Mme. Tussaud's world-renowned collection of wax figures. First one passes through various galleries in which skillful reproductions of kings, cabinet ministers, movie stars, generals, aviators, cricket players, presidents (including Warren Gamaliel Harding), little old ladies and attendants (spotted about in lifelike stances among real visitors) may be admired. But for 7d [seven pence] extra one is admitted into the "Chamber of Horrors" in the basement. There are ancient relics of torture, miniature dioramas depicting medieval executions, and a number of wax figures representing famous murderers, all of whom look exceedingly respectable and inconspicuous. Their descriptions in the catalogue run like this:

"Samuel H. Dougal. Executed 1903 for the Moat Farm Murder.

"George Chapman. Executed 1903 for the murder of three barmaids.

"Johann Schneider. Executed in 1899 for the murder of a baker.

"Henry Fowler and Albert Milsom. Executed in 1896 for the murder of an aged gentleman at Muswell Hill." Etc. etc.

This "Chamber of Horrors"—the horrors of the Sunday supplement—amuses me hugely. How inconsequential and trivial a Victorian axe murder seems in the perspective of today's great carnage—millions and millions of human beings scientifically tortured and butchered in a vale of complete anonymity. So great an anonymity, in fact, that right in London's Hyde Park there are speakers who urge England to "get rid of the Jews." As long as there's one left alive the ills of the world will be placed on his shoulders, and when he's dead a new one will have to be invented to serve the function.

I visited Hyde Park again Friday night, after the opera. The meetings were already petering out, and the Irishmen were coming into their own. They come out there in the darkness and gather in little crowds to sing songs of their homeland, including much that is I.R.A. and Sinn Fein.

In London I went to see a satirical political musical performed by a small troupe of actors who had somehow evaded military service. Their big number ended with a refrain addressed to Ernest Bevin, the labor minister and long-time union leader. The ditty went, "Ernie, Ernie, when we've won the war, are we going back on the dole?"

At Ascot, one evening, a lieutenant colonel in charge of troop morale set up a lecture on the post-war world by Lord Vansittart, known for his aggressive opposition to Nazism before the war. He spoke informally, sitting down in an armchair, to several dozen of us who chose this rather than a movie. The questions all started with "Sir!" Afterwards I overheard the speaker tell the colonel that he had found the discussion with the enlisted men far more intelligent than the one that followed his talk to the officers a few days earlier. "Oh, it's always like that," the colonel said laconically.

The V-1 buzz bombs, a powerful self-destructing unmanned-aircraft type of German weapon, were raining down on London at that time, especially after dark. As they were first spotted crossing the North Sea, sirens sounded in the city, followed by the rasping noise of the motors, then a deathly silence followed by a resounding explosion. Although one was supposed to seek shelter from these attacks, which were directed mainly at the center and eastern parts of the city, many people ignored them. In a military-occupied hotel in Mayfair, I fell asleep amidst the din and went down the next morning to a dining room filled with sunshine and the glorious optimistic sounds of Ralph Vaughn Williams's "London Symphony" over amplifiers set to the BBC.

Folkestone

We came under more closely directed enemy fire when our newly formed signal intelligence unit began practice exercises in the coastal city of Folkestone, which was subjected to periodic shelling. The German installations were only a few miles away across the Dover straits in Calais, whose coast we could clearly see from the Kentish cliffs. We would stand on the esplanade and watch the bright flashes of the guns, followed by explosions on our side of the water. It was disconcerting, both in Folkestone and nearby Dover, to walk or drive by bombed-out residences that we had seen intact just the day before. In spite of the harassment and danger, the English continued for the most part in the grooves of their normal lives. In my hours off I could take a red doubledecker bus along the coast to Hastings or Deal, or inland to Canterbury, badly damaged a few years earlier by conventional bombing raids. (I encountered the buzz bombs again a few months later in Liège, Belgium, to which they brought extensive havoc and the lingering sound of shattered glass.) We left England just as the V-1s were joined by the terrible V-2, Wernher von Braun's rocket bomb, which moved too fast for any prior warning.[5]

Folkestone, September 6, 1944: Now I live in a former civilian residence in a small English city. The room which I share with two other fellows was formerly a children's nursery. It has canary-colored walls covered with pictures of Snow White and the Seven Dwarfs, and we have added our own maps of the battle zone by way of decoration. Running water and electric lights make this much more comfortable than the cold damp tents in which I've been staying.

Canterbury, September 12, 1944: There's nothing in it of the slightest significance from a military viewpoint. The Germans gave it the full blitz in '41. They evidently tried to destroy the cathedral, but only got the precious libraries on its grounds, and they razed many blocks of historic buildings. But nothing that they do is capable of analysis by any normal human standards.

Signal Intelligence

Our unit was Detachment D of the 3rd Radio Squadron Mobile (G), whose code name was "Flap." Our military name, "Flap Dog,"[6] somehow resonated better than those of our sister detachments, "Flap Able," "Flap Baker," and "Flap Charlie," which served the other Tactical Air Commands that supported the operations of the First, Third, and Seventh Armies. We were attached to the 19th TAC, whose fighter planes backed up the Ninth Army. (After the liberation of France, this army was positioned on the front between Montgomery's British forces to the north and the U.S. First Army to the south.)

Our mission was to provide intelligence on German air activity, by listening in on the Luftwaffe's radio communications.[7] We eavesdropped on what the enemy's ground controllers were telling their pilots and on what the pilots were telling them and each other. We could do this because in that era voice signals could not easily be garbled and reassembled, as can now be done. Both on our side and the enemy's, audio messages were sent "in the clear," like any normal broadcast or telephone conversation. The assumption was that in the heat of battle, instant communication was more important than security from monitoring by the other side.

We listened at half a dozen receivers, a few of them retrieved from shot-down German aircraft, and the others designed to cover the same frequency range.

These were manned around the clock by four shifts of operators whose German ranged from native to barely acceptable. (In my case it was serviceable.) We worked roughly from 7 A.M. to 1 P.M., went back from 7 to midnight, from 1 to 7 the following afternoon, and the next day took nocturnal duty from midnight to 7.

In addition to the van in which we worked, there was a headquarters van, where the officer on duty communicated over a ground telephone line to the 19th TAC ground control, located at an airfield some distance away. (It was in the resort town of Spa during our sojourn in Belgium. We were supposed to be as close to the front lines as we could get without incurring danger of coming under enemy small-arms fire.) Two other vans housed our direction-finding equipment. One was located near us, and the other far enough away so that, by rotating antennas to bring in a radio signal as clearly as possible, its source could be located through triangulation.

About a third of the one-hundred-man complement of Flap Dog was made up of German-language specialists; the remainder were technicians (radio and switchboard operators and maintenance men), and support personnel—drivers, cooks, guards, and clerks. (To avoid the onerous duties of KP, all of us contributed to a kitty that supplemented the pay of some of the men in this last category, and they cheerfully took on the dishwashing and other scullery chores.) Except for the detachment commander, Lt. Ferdinand Gottlieb, none of our four officers was fluent in German. One knew some Norwegian and one was a native speaker of Yiddish; in the eyes of higher authorities these apparently seemed like sufficiently similar languages to qualify them for this secret intelligence work.

Our *modus operandi* in the radio van was to keep twirling the dial in the frequency band used by the Luftwaffe. At any sign of activity several of us followed it while others continued to search, because often a number of actions were under way simultaneously. We had to coordinate with the direction-finding crew, who tried to pinpoint the source of the signals. We called out what we heard to our team leader, who called it in to the headquarters van; the officer on duty relayed it in turn to the TAC control officer, who alerted our aircraft—both the fighters based on the continent, and the bombers of the 8th Air Force, based in the United Kingdom. As we called out what we heard, we also wrote it down. These logs were forwarded to the Royal Air Force signal intelligence analysts at an English manor house, who assembled all the available data about the Luftwaffe.

Much of the time, the voices we overheard were those of Luftwaffe ground personnel warning of Allied air activity— *"dicke Autos"* (fat bombers) or *"Indianer"* (fighters). Their own planes were *"kleine Freunde"* (little friends, just what we called our fighters). Sometimes controllers at widely separated airports spoke openly to each other. The most exciting moments came when the Germans sent their dwindling air resources up to waylay our bombers or to attack our fighters.

The conversations were short and frantic. Pilots would announce that they were attacking, gloat that they had just made a kill *(ein Abschuss)*, shout that they were short of fuel, that their plane had been hit, that they were bailing out. Occasionally their last utterance was a piercing scream. And sometimes such actions were going on at several places simultaneously and overheard at different points on the dial. Then the team leader and the duty officer had to try to sort out what was going on.

The leader of my team was Sgt. Sidney Axelrod, an old man of thirty-nine whose birth date had made him, only by a few days, eligible for the draft—a misfortune that he never ceased to lament. "The Axe" had been a medical student in Switzerland before the war, lodging in a rooming house that was, as he told us with a nostalgic sigh, *sturmfrei*, or accessible to brief female visitations.

Wherever I was, there were always individuals over whose heads the war seemed to pass, who made no social overtures and few friends, who managed to keep out of trouble and who seemed destined to return unscathed to their civilian lives. In Flap Dog there was Corporal Blake, always reserved, formal, and well-mannered amidst the raw vulgarity of the surrounding soldiery. Blake had been a teacher at one of the elite boarding schools in Massachusetts. He was gaunt, and like many extremely tall people, walked with a stoop as though to make himself inconspicuous.

On the night shifts, when activity was scant, there was, in fact, much reminiscence of prewar life. For those of our crew who were refugees from Hitler's Germany, the pre-army American experience had been a brief one. A recent emigré from Vienna regaled us endlessly with descriptions of his favorite coffee houses, where one could retire for hours with a *Kaffee mit Schlag* (coffee with whipped cream) or a *Jause* (substantial snack) and study a variety of newspapers. The subject of food came up repeatedly in these nocturnal conversations, with vivid descriptions of Mom's great specialties and memorable restaurant meals.

Tuning In

As we searched the radio band devoted to German military communications, we could hardly avoid exposure to the ordinary broadcasts that breached the military front lines and political boundaries of wartime Europe.

When we first started out in Folkestone, and for some time after we arrived in France, we could hear the BBC's French-language programs interrupted by coded messages, some carrying real instructions to the fighters of the Maquis, others undoubtedly intended to confound our counterparts, the Germans who were trying to make sense of them. The most ubiquitous signals came from the "Great German Radio with All of Its Transmitters," which offered an almost steady stream of Wagnerian opera sung by golden and heroic voices. (Papageno's *Glockenspiel* theme from "The Magic Flute" signaled a break between programs.) The domestic news programs referred derisively to the "terror bombers" assailing their cities. The Germans also served up English-language news broadcasts that mimicked the BBC style, with announcers who used impeccable Oxbridge diction that deceived the cooks and drivers of our unit. The contents were cleverly selected to include a mixture of truth and lies intended to sap the morale of Allied listeners. They had their pseudo-documentaries; when the Soviets began their final counter-offensive, the Wehrmacht held out at a bastion in Estonia, and in broadcasts, ostensibly from the front, the announcer's voice competed with the sounds of rifle-fire and exploding shells. "*Vor Narwa*," he proclaimed portentously, "*steht Europa!*" ("In front of Narva stands Europe!")

The Soviets too, had their German-language programming, some openly declaring, "*Hier ist Moskau*," while others masqueraded under guises like the Voice of Austrian Resistance. This type of deceptively attributed "black" propaganda was especially entertaining. The British operated a *Soldatensender* (soldier transmitter) *West* that featured an "old top sergeant" who was easy to visualize as a character out of *Woyzeck* or maybe *The Captain from Koepenick*. In crusty tones, *der alte Feldwebel* spoke out against the universal failings of military bureaucracy and kept reminding his listeners in the Wehrmacht that the jig was up and that they had best cut and run to surrender at their first chance.

The Russians not only broadcast the news to their own troops at a normal speed; at certain times they also broadcast the same items at a molasses-slow pace, so that the Party commissar in each military unit could copy it down to be mimeographed or printed for the benefit of those without radios.

We listened to the stirring speeches of Churchill and to Hitler's rantings. At war's end we heard Adm. Alfred Doenitz tell the German people and armed forces of his surrender. The voices crackling over the air gave me the feeling that all of Europe, occupied and free, was at my fingertips. The censored news reports that came from the American Armed Forces Radio Network and the BBC could be compared with what the multi-tongued voices of German propaganda were saying. As the news poured out in a constant flow, we updated the map on which we charted the front and had the deluded sensation that we were abreast of what the best-informed generals knew about the war's course. Although we were not in direct combat, we had the sense that we were in the thick of things. But all of this was yet to come.

Chapter 6

On the Continent

When the time came for us to cross the Channel from Weymouth to Omaha Beach, we loaded our trucks on to an LST (Landing Ship, Tanks), and braved the rolling seas that made most of us violently seasick. Because of tides and rough weather, we spent four days on this ship (only one day at sea) before we could disembark. Even three months after D-Day, the beach was littered with military debris, which was being cleared by hundreds of green-uniformed prisoners. Among them were exotic-looking men from Central Asia who had switched sides as recruits to the Nazi-created anti-Soviet Russian Army of Gen. Vassily Vlasov.

Normandy, September, 1944: I can mention the kids in England who give you solemn V-signs as your truck approaches the Port of Embarkation, and I can go into glorious ecstasies over the little, undernourished children of France, who wave frantically at you from all the windows along all the roads. There are sights I would like to tell you about which are miracles and manifestations of the war and of our army, as such can't be talked about. But I can say that I've seen battlefields and destruction unimaginable to anyone who hasn't seen it. I am afraid of breaking into clichés. The descriptions that would be censored if I attempted to give them have appeared a thousand times in great detail in the papers at home. I can only say amen, give assent and affirmation to their truisms—towns razed to the ground, reduced to a common denominator of dusty white rubble. If a wall still stands it bears the ubiquitous, long-banned tricolor. And—from where they come I can't imagine—there are still civilians poking about for salvage in the ruins, civilians who still have the time to wave occasionally at the stream of G.I. trucks that passes them.

My momentary location was formerly a German billet, and I have a huge stack of newspapers, magazines and other miscellany to wade through. It gives one a queer feeling to see their pin up girls, their half-used bottles of hair oil, the beautiful slick paper of Goebbels' *Das Reich* and to realize that the veneer of civilized amenity cloaks barbarism and cruelty of a fiendish order.[1]

The stories one hears from the French are in no way different from the tales we had heard at home. A kid of 19 (he looks like 15) on his way to join the new

French army tells of his torture by the SS. One passes a great public building and one's companion remarks casually that the Germans caught 200 Maquis and burnt them alive there. Someone else managed to escape from an ambush but his friends had their hands and ears hacked off. Somebody's brother, a boy of 18, hung a dead chicken on a pole with the sign, "I'd rather be dead than lay eggs for the Germans." Shot. The workman in the railway yard tells of the machine gun that the Nazis used to keep men on their toes, and *used*.

But most poignant for me thus far has been this: We walk down the street of a little town at night, my friend Barney [Kruglak] and I. Toward us comes a gang of little kids, singing brightly. I holler out in what would be accepted by any American or English kids as a kidding tone that it's pretty late at night to be holding a song fest in the streets. Suddenly there is a horrible and terrified silence, and with a sudden flash of insight I realize that for those kids Barney and I are dark shapes in uniform, that for the four main years of their lives dark shapes in uniforms have meant Boches [derogatory French term for Germans], and that when the Boche in the street shouted at the kids there was no love or humor in his voice, and if one got in his way, or made too much noise, or didn't leave the sidewalk when he came along, one could be kicked to the gutter or shot stone dead, whether one was seven or seventy.

Oh, I called to the kids, I laughed and told them that when the Boches said things like that one had to believe them, but that it's different now. And then they were suddenly alive and cheerful and shrilly gay again and clustered around us shaking our hands. (The inevitable first question after I address someone in French: *"Alors, vous êtes français, monsieur."* ["So you're French, Sir."] *"Pas du tout, je suis Américain."* ["Not at all, I'm American."] *"Mais vous parlez très bien, comme un Français!"* ["But you speak very well, like a Frenchman."]) Barney and I start handing out our precious reserves of candy, sugar, chewing gum. (One stick divided eight ways). I ask them where they're going. One of them shows me. He has a can of milk, half full. *"C'est pour toi?"* ["Is that for you?"] *"Non, c'est pour ma petite soeur."* ["No, it's for my little sister."] (He himself is about six years old, but even bread is rationed in France. "The minimum number of daily calories to live on," a Frenchman described the situation to me, but everyone is agreed that things are much better since the liberation.)

"Dans quelle classe es-tu a l'école?" [What class are you in at school?] I ask a little girl. *"La classe de Mme. Duval,"* she replies brightly. *"Mais naturellement, Mme. Duval,"* I say, with the wise smile of the omniscient grown-up. Kids! The bloodthirsty chap of eight or so who exclaims excitedly, *"Vous allez faire aux Boches comme ça!"* ["You're going to do this to the Germans!"] His hand slices across his neck expressively and his throat makes an unappetizing sound. I translate for Barney, who says, "Oh, oui, oui," and points menacingly to his trench knife.

That is France, that is a people and a land and a culture which I already love, and which is maligned here and at home by the same people who hate England and the "Limeys" for the same reason—because its spirit and meaning escape and bewilder them. I stand on a corner with my friend. Across the street a thin little girl is playing. After a few minutes she runs across the street to us and gravely shakes our hands. *"Je suis bien contente de vous voir ici, messieurs."* ["I'm very happy to see you here, gentlemen."] France, age eight.

And France is the two young civilians, former French soldiers and war prisoners in Germany, who spent a whole evening traipsing about to show us some of the life that Elliot Paul's book on the French scene *[The Last Time I Saw Paris]* describes with such warmth—and who then wanted to pay for our drinks. (By the way, in any small French town after dark, which comes quite early now, the only forms of entertainment are the café, the brothel and in some cases the cinema. Which is a decided encouragement to the potential loose livers among us.) And France is the family who practically forced delicious apples and peaches upon us and drove us almost "home," ten miles out of their way, in their charcoal-burning auto.

Sure, France is other things and people too. It's the gamins who hang around Army posts and collect small fortunes in cigarettes and candy, which they store in sacks. And it's the old hag whose sour *"Que fais-tu avec les foux Américains?"* ["What are you doing with those crazy Americans?"] to a kid talking with some G.I.s turns to a false smile of ingratiation when I interject that *"nous ne sommes pas exactement des foux, madame!"* [We're not altogether crazy, lady."] *"Alors, vous êtes français, vous!"* ["So you're French!"] etc. But there's an élan and a vitality and a beauty here that makes me understand the American artist expatriates after the last war with a sympathy that I could never before muster, and perhaps a tinge of envy.

September 30, 1944: Our living conditions have varied from the most primitive shifting for ourselves to what by present standards approaches luxury. One night we may be sleeping on the ground or in trucks with our blankets and tent canvas wrapped around us, with K or C rations for our food. (K comes in one little package about $1" \times 8" \times 3"$, containing a can of meat or powdered egg or cheese, powdered beverage, cigarettes, toilet paper, candy and biscuits and sugar. C consists of two cans, one of which has crackers, candy, beverage (powdered) and sugar, the other one of which is a meat and vegetable stew which can be eaten either cold or hot; it's heated over a fire produced in a similar can which one half-fills with dirt and soaks in gasoline.) And the next night we may be living like "kings" aboard ship, with warm cots and excellent food. At present we're living in quarters formerly inhabited by the Germans, and though they destroyed some of the vital facilities before they left, we're still quite comfortable compared to the infantrymen sleeping in the muddy fields.

Some of the wrecked towns I've seen are so sickening that one can't even smile as one waves back to the French who wave at one from the side of the road. Every house, wrecked or intact, has a tricolor hanging from its window, and occasionally homemade British and American flags. The kids are already used to us, though. They wear G.I. shoulder patches and ask for chewing gum in a most accomplished manner. And do they *hate* the Boches! People in America have no idea of what the Germans are like, but these people have lived under them for four years, slaved for them, been tortured and pillaged by them. The memories are still fresh and vivid. Unfortunately by the time I'm off duty it's almost dark, and at nightfall everything shuts up tight and goes to bed. But this is still an enormous adventure, and there's no sign of boredom ahead of me.

I haven't seen a newspaper. Curious that you in America should know all about what's happening while we in a zone of operations are completely in the dark about it. I don't know yet whether I can send home any German printed matter, which is on beautiful slick paper and full of toothpaste ads that make one frantically unable to comprehend how a nation that brushes its teeth twice a day also annihilates whole populations with methodical savagery and uses the cremated remains for fertilizer. This war is far from won, don't kid yourselves. People at home, people in England, don't realize how big a job it is to win it.

We drove through the razed towns and villages of Normandy, where the invasion had proceeded inch by inch and finally established our billets in the chateau of La Jonchère at Bougival, in the western suburbs of Paris. Not by coincidence, this had been the site of our counterpart unit in the Luftwaffe.

Although a number of weeks had passed since the liberation of Paris on August 25, there was much talk of pockets of resistance by die-hard German troops and their *Milice* collaborators.[2] Occasional shots were heard, probably set off by nervous Americans or their Allies. We shivered somewhat at the thought that some former Luftwaffe occupants of our chateau might still be holed up in the vicinity. A nearby cave, part of which may have served as a bomb shelter, seemed like a plausible hide-out, and several of us ventured to explore its depths. We had gone several hundred feet when we heard a tap-tap-tapping in the distance. We extinguished our flashlights and released the safety catches of our carbines, ready to fire. The tapper turned out to be a little old woman with a basket on her arm, who became alarmed at our sudden appearance. "*Je cueille des champignons, messieurs*," ["I'm gathering mushrooms, gentlemen,"] she explained.

We carried our helmets and carbines on our first few trips into Paris, but discovered that we stood out among the soldiers who had already converted to unarmed garrison dress. We had been warned about the lubricious attractions of "Pig Alley" (Place Pigalle), with its movie theaters, brasseries, and ambulatory prostitutes, but on my first daytime visit, it seemed altogether tame and dull.

Our detachment commander, Lieutenant Gottlieb, was himself an emigré from Germany. He felt that we were getting sloppy in the midst of our Parisian distractions. While we stood at attention in parade formation, he lectured us on the importance of proper appearance. "I vant you should look like dolls, phallus [fellows]." Then he disappeared for a few days, heading for the front in search of a suitable location for our operations.

October 23, 1944: If you get to Paris, go to see Picasso at 7, Rue des Grands Augustins. I missed his great new exhibition by one day, and couldn't see his studio work because I came in the evening when it was blacked out. He is simple, pleasant, courteous—just what one would expect from a man of his genius. (You know of course of his work with the Resistance during the occupation.) [In fact, Picasso's wartime record was not admirable.] Incidentally, he uses the standard Paris slum latrine which consists of a big round hole in the floor through which everything goes.

I had gone around to Picasso's place several times on the few occasions when I was able to get a ride into Paris from Bougival, but he was out on my earlier visits. The concierge told me that another American had also come by that day. "A Monsieur Hemingway. Do you know him?" Picasso asked whether I painted; I told him I wrote "a little." He expressed interest in the volume I had just bought at a booth by the Seine, the essays of Montaigne, and said they were charming. His paintings, he explained, were all at his studio, and he gave me the address and invited me to come by. But when I returned to our chateau I found we had just been given the orders to move up to the front in Belgium the following day.

Chapter 7

On the Heels of the Wehrmacht

We moved out in several stages. I was fortunate enough to be in a truck commanded by the Yiddish-speaking lieutenant, who routed us through Reims so that we could admire the cathedral, destroyed by artillery in World War I, restored with Rockefeller money, and now damaged again as the Germans retreated. Our destination was Arlon, a small city in Southeastern Belgium, just across the border from Luxembourg.

Arlon

Arlon, October, 1944: This Belgian town squats amidst a rolling green fertility of fields and pine forests. Seen from the distance it appears as one great compact lump, crowned with the spires of its churches and public buildings. Its ancient streets wind weird irregular spirals around the central square. Their cobblestones have borne the boots of soldiers from a dozen nations and a dozen centuries. We are only the latest invaders, but unlike most of the others we have come as friends and allies, and the Belgians are not likely to forget that. The Germans, who preceded us, were more in the medieval tradition of murder and arson. One night two Belgian officials, a lawyer and a doctor, were dragged off to the Gestapo torture chambers (a roomy comfortable house on a side street), "questioned," and released in the morning. When they reached the main street on their way home they were shot in the back and lay painfully dying in the gutter, one for eight hours, the other for six, with no one permitted to give aid. It is little things like this that make most Europeans dislike the Germans. (The fine distinction between Nazis and good peace-loving fundamentally democratic German soldiers, SS men and Gestapo agents is not generally drawn in these parts.)

One afternoon I took a walk, got slightly lost, and thus discovered the town synagogue, which bore no indications of former function on its grey stone exterior, other than the austere Byzantine curves that also mark the masonry of Lower East Side prayer houses in New York. The building was small, for the town's Jewish population was never more than 200 or so. Inside there was a balcony, Orthodox style, for the women, and in the rear of the balcony a tattered plush canopy marked the place where the choir stood and sang. On the wall high above the altar the Ten Commandments tablet stood untouched. Also intact was the suspended red "eternal" lamp, long extinguished. Everything else in the nature of religious articles, decorations and furnishings had been torn, smashed or stolen.

But this is not what I noticed when I entered, for the sight of the desecrated altar and ravaged walls is only an appropriately rugged shell for the greater horror that the hall contains. Towering up to the high ceiling is a great pile of furniture. It is all mixed up and disorderly, like a heap of rubbish, or better still, like a pile of bodies in the pictures of the Germans' mass graves in the East. There is furniture that is modern and new beneath its layer of dust and some that has been owned by the same family for many generations. There are babies' cribs and kitchen chairs and long extensible dining room tables. And sofas, beds, chiffoniers, china closets: the full simple gamut of accessories to the household life of simple people. This furniture belonged to the Jews of the town who were sent to Poland to be slaughtered.

The old Belgian caretaker of the synagogue spoke of this very shortly and with a great angry quiver in his voice. One doesn't talk of such things. It was something whose meaning he couldn't understand and that I couldn't understand. Maybe some day someone will be able to understand it, not by any intellectual comprehension of the causes, theory and practice of the Fascist psychosis, but innerly, from within the blurry roaring musical fog of the Fascist brain.

The Jews were loaded at night on a train of cattle freight cars. All of them, said the caretaker. They didn't take anything with them. The rabbi was a man in his eighties. He had a long white beard, wore a dignified black frock coat, and his person and counsel were much respected by the elders of the town. At the railroad station (it is quite a nice one, with a large news stand and a restaurant and signs in German to help out the Nazi soldiers and officials passing through) the rabbi suffered a stroke and died. His body was flung into the car along with the living. "Like the carcass of a pig," said the caretaker, and his hands trembled. "They are savage beasts," growled the old man. "They are beasts, not human beings."

When the Jewish community was sent away the Belgians managed to save a few children and smuggled them off to stay with peasants in the country. One of them was a little boy of about eight years, who was put in the care of a woman in a village a few miles away. One day, several months later, the foster-mother received an apparently routine notice to bring the child in for inoculation, with what turned out to be poison. The people simply cannot understand what Germany gained by the death of this child.

October 15, 1944: The people here in town have been very nice to us. I've visited with three families and had dinner with one. The menu: pea soup, pumpernickel bread and butter, cognac, beer, salad of cole slaw, hard boiled eggs and ham, roast rabbit (which looks and tastes exactly like chicken or turkey), French fried potatoes, carrots and peas, apple pie (not very good, because there's so little sugar and shortening) and coffee. Don't draw from this the conclusion that everyone here eats like this all the time. It's a tough struggle here to get food. A woman I know walks miles and miles into the country to get fresh eggs (at $1 a half dozen) for her little boy.[1] Sometimes at night when we're very hungry we engage in long luxurious discussions of the things we'd like to eat now, things "Momma used to make," from noodle soup to strawberry shortcake, from strudel to chopped liver.

A Visit to Luxembourg

Arlon, October 20, 1944: The night before the one just past was spent at work, the morning afterwards in the restful gloomy purgatory of the sack. Then noontime, lunch, and Bob Strotz to take me away to his fortuitously discovered relatives not very far from here. The combination of extended thumb and passing G.I. traffic was good for transportation most of the way; the remaining five kilometers we hiked along a winding road past pleasant fields and steep slopes covered with dense pine forests whose trees had been planted in neat rows with Teutonic accuracy.

The village [Bondorf, in the Grand Duchy of Luxembourg] in which Bob's forebears dwelt is like most in this area. It's about a mile and a half from the main road and nestles in a pretty valley; sun gleams on its slate roofs and on the spire of its church. (Individual isolated farm houses are unknown in Western Europe. The peasants clustered their houses together, originally for protection in the medieval pattern. Since European agriculture is intensive and distances relatively small by American standards, the advantages of this communal life far outweigh the trouble of walking back and forth from the fields.)

The dominating feature of the village is the sight, odor and universal squashed stickiness of dung underfoot. Down the streets and lanes there is an almost endless procession of fat lethargic pigeon-toed cattle, whose trail of droppings, accumulated for centuries, has been mashed and mixed with the muddy thoroughfare. In addition to this, every peasant house has its own pretentious dung-pile (whose size is an accurate index of family prosperity) just outside the door. Stables are an integral part of the family dwelling. This economizes on construction costs and saves fuel in the winter too. The housewife who wishes to prepare fresh eggs needs only to open her kitchen door and reach into the adjacent hen roost for the family breakfast. When the door is open, the house is filled with lowing, baahing, clucking, crowing, quacking and other pleasant barnyard sounds.

Bob had already been here last week to visit his various second, third and fourth degree cousins. We stopped at the outskirts of the village to ask directions of some kids. (Kids are wonderful and the same in every country.) They rushed, giggling-solemn, to show us the way. New recruits arrived from every house and alleyway, and we arrived at the home of Bob's "principal" cousin at the head of a large, proud procession.

Our reception was fabulously splendid. It appeared that the whole village was in one way or another related to the Strotzes, and more and more horny-handed peasants and bashful children kept arriving to crowd into the little living room and shake the hands of the missing link with the family from overseas.

We were regaled with liqueurs, beer and unending glasses of Mosel wine. No sooner had we arrived, in fact, than the table was spread and we were fed with fresh fried eggs (my first since England), hard-boiled egg and lettuce salad, crisp roasted baby potatoes, ham with parsley, cake and cookies. In the course of the afternoon, we visited three or four other houses, so that Bob might admire ancient photographs of long-deceased ancestors, and there again hospitality overflowed.

The people spoke their own patois among themselves, but our communication with them proceeded quite nicely. They had the usual song of hate to sing against "the Prussians," and explained how for the four years of the occupation, the kids returning from school recited their lessons for the family and received strenuous contradiction of the same.[2] That is one of the most amazing and encouraging things I have noticed in formerly occupied regions—the people never resigned themselves to what at one time must have appeared inevitable; they continued to hope, and in this hope to bring up their children in contradiction to the official dogmas. All of which speaks to the relative influence of domestic and formal education in the conditioning process.

Two distant relatives of Bob's had been forced into the Wehrmacht at pistol-point as "volunteers," had fought and been wounded in Russia, and had deserted while on furlough, six months before the Allied invasion. They were now serving in the local militia. Their descriptions of the Russian campaign (they had been in the Caucasus in '42) tallied perfectly with the picture we know—fierce unmitigated hatred, deadly effective partisan activity by the Russians. They opined that there was a considerable amount of disaffection in the German Army, but all on a disorganized individual basis. And of course *everyone*, including these "Communists" in the German Army, regardless of any opposition to Hitler and the Nazis, wants Germany to win the war. Oh yes, and one of these guys was around one day when the SS shot 20,000 Jews. I asked him whether the average German soldier was completely indifferent to this sort of thing and he sort of shrugged his shoulders and remarked that there was a cleavage between the Army and the Party.

These two brothers had been serving in different, separated organizations. Both were wounded at the same time, one in the wrist and the other by a piece of shrapnel that passed through his scalp and came out of his mouth, knocking out great numbers of teeth in the process. By a curious coincidence they landed in the same hospital in adjacent beds (probably for alphabetical reasons.) The one with the head wound was completely bandaged except for his eyes and nose. Though he recognized his brother he couldn't communicate with him, whereas the one in the next bed never realized that the wrapped-up creature was his brother. Eventually they made contact.

I also made further discoveries about the German occupation of Belgium:

I paid a visit several evenings ago to one of the few Jewish families who escaped the Nazis in [Arlon]. They had been hidden in a farm house in the country for the past two years. My initial hope was that they would help round out my picture of Fascism, but I realized quickly that their sorrows were too great to be expressed, that all memories and fears had to be pushed away—far far out of the orbit of consciousness—that to remain sane one had to live in present circumstances—this room, this table, stove, dress, bowl of apples on the table. One old lady in a black dress brought out a picture of her niece, who was "in Poland." "She is seventeen now; she was only 15 when they took her away. I haven't heard from her since then. It's been two years." It was a sepia-tinted studio photograph of a plain-faced young girl in an old-fashioned "grown-up" long dress, against a painted scenic backdrop. There is more horror for me in that simple photograph, in that old woman's pathetic conviction that the reality of the picture somehow invokes the reality of her niece's continuing life, than there would be in the full story of the girl's torture, rape and murder. That is what I fear the aftermath of the Hitler terror will resolve itself into: individuals carrying the snapshots and infant hair locks of the dead in their pocketbooks. Nowhere purgation, nowhere resolution, nowhere the decisive slashing of knots long and laboriously tied.

In Arlon, there was a small mulatto boy who had been mocked by the German troops when they were in residence. There were also assorted peasant maidens, with ruddy faces, stout legs, and broad bottoms, whose acquaintance was cultivated by some of our crew. One afternoon, I saw one of these girls emerging tearfully from the house in which our drivers were billeted. They were shouting curses at her and telling her to beat it. Only years later, when I thought about this episode, did I realize that I had witnessed the aftermath of a gang rape.
  By contrast, another sexual conquest was gleefully publicized by its author, Hans Knauth, a Midwesterner originally from Halle an der Saale, where his mother still lived. A chambermaid who unexpectedly entered the room in which he was sleeping was enticed to his bed in order to tuck him in, and allowed herself to be seduced in short order. Short indeed, because he enjoyed repeating her punch line: *"Ist ihre Natur schon gekommen, Herr Knauth?"* **("Has your nature**

come yet, Mr. Knauth?") (Months later, apropos of the genial Knauth, I received a strong put-down from a German PW. He said, *"Sie sprechen die deutsche Sprache, aber Er* (pointing to Knauth) *spricht deutsches Dialekt."* ("You speak the German language, but *he* speaks German dialect.")

Luxembourg Prison

Luxembourg city, October, 1944: This monstrous ugly ancient prison was once crowded with Gestapo victims and is now full of Nazis awaiting punishment for their crimes. I got there in the usual fortuitous way. Irv [Rosow] and I had been told by a policeman of an interesting medieval chapel that had been a great tourist attraction before the war. ("Oh, how the Englishmen used to throw their money away here!") It's amazing how the removal of a language barrier breeds cordiality and intimacy with strangers. We stood at a crossroads and asked further directions. As always the person we asked insisted on going out of his way to show us around, and in fact to put himself at our disposal for any further sightseeing, since he had "nothing else to do." He was a dark-haired, thin-featured young man of 25 or so, who wore the worn brown jacket and baggy grey pants of the Western European worker, with a silk print muffler around his neck in lieu of a collar and tie. We began our excursion like the Pied Piper of Hamelin, with two pretty little children, a girl and a boy of 6 or 7, clinging excitedly to our hands and jabbering away in their patois, which we couldn't understand, though they could understand us. (That to me is one of the real tests of the effects of German occupation; a woman remarked to me how strange it was; the children always completely ignored the German soldiers, whereas they chase after Americans to shake hands and have their heads patted. This despite the last four years of Nazi-controlled education.) Unfortunately their escapade ended unhappily for the little girl at least, because her Mama began looking for her and spanking her before we could explain that it was our fault. Then Mama tried to pet and make up to her darling, who kept on bawling miserably over the great injustice.

Our guide was from a little country village some distance from here; his peacetime occupation was tailor; during the war he had worked in a garage in town. For four years he had been a member of the Underground—he showed me his "passport" in the movement, a printed document on pink paper complete with photograph and seal. Despite the sizable proportion of collaborators and pro-Nazis in the local population he estimated that most of the youth as well as many older people were actively connected with the Resistance movement. He had been arrested by the Gestapo and held for fourteen months in the local jail—two months on charges and twelve on general principles. Now the tables were turned. He was a militiaman and prison guard in the same jail in which he had formerly been captive.

So we went to this old prison, initially to see its medieval chapel, in the center of which a full partition separated the pews of the petty criminals from those of the lifers and men sentenced to death. (This was in peacetime. There are only political prisoners there now.) Perhaps it was strange for two unknown G.I.s to receive permission of the prison superintendent to be shown about its inner precincts, but this is a strange time and place. The prison guards included the old-timers in their gaudy pre-war uniforms and the members of the popular militia, young workers like our friend, wearing no uniform except for the armbands on their sleeves. Things were still roughly organized. For the first two weeks after liberation, in fact, an audacious young Nazi, masquerading as a representative of the government in exile, had assumed control of the whole works and had almost managed to sabotage them until he was found out.

The guards lived inside the prison walls in a barracks as crowded and austere as the cells themselves. They lived in the essence of the past four years and in the glorious moment of retribution and self-assertion. Beyond the numerous gates that closed ponderously behind us and were locked shut as we made our way into the buildings, were the lively streets of a town full of black-stockinged young matrons wheeling clean pink babies in perambulators, brisk, clean-shaven businessmen wearing black homburg hats and briefcases, pretty girls and kids on bicycles—the busy bourgeois world of buy and sell and go to church that goes on and on through war and peace and fall of governments. But here in the depths of the prison was the ugly core on which all the tranquility falsely rested.

The prison cells were large and packed with beds. There were bed rolls in the corridors too, to take care of the overflow. There were horrid little cells, 4' × 8' × 6' or so, which the Nazis had used for solitary confinement; the chains were still there.

We stood at a staircase landing and suddenly from below there came a roar and the shuffling of many feet. The prisoners were being led up to their cells. Now they came up past us, curious, shifty-eyed. These were not the mere pro-Germans of the region; they were the active workers, the Gestapo spies and stool pigeons, the grafters, murderers, the imported vampires and bureaucrats. They wore the civilian clothes in which they had been arrested, they wore a tired stubborn evil on their faces. They were mostly middle-aged men; they looked like bank clerks, storekeepers. Here and there was a cocky youngster of 19 or 21, with long curly hair slicked back, black horn-rimmed goggles, the Western European equivalent of a zoot suit. These were the ones who looked at us squarely; they were more dangerous. Did they still believe in a German victory?

Outdoors in the prison yard there were more of them, taking their exercise with bowed heads, and an endless spiral walk at six pace intervals. They do not smile; the prosperous-looking gent in the dark wool coat and the leather gloves; is he thinking, or is he simply still a little dazed to realize that his time is up? The ferret-faced long-nosed chap in the green felt hat up front—he looks like a Hollywood Nazi—he has the death of 20 patriots on his head. Shall one weep a tear for them or for the others? The young militiaman in the jacket two sizes too small for him, who was introduced to me as a deserter from the German army, shouts at them to move it along. I ask what punishment awaits these men and get a shrug of the shoulders in reply. One doesn't know, one must wait for the end of the war. This is a peaceable land, one that is strong for traditions.

Now here is a prison guard who has been in Germany for the last three years, until September 7. He was in Frankfurt-am-Main, which was 60% destroyed when he left, and there have been two heavy air raids since. Yes, they are tired of the war up there, they know it's lost, but they are afraid, afraid of the walls and floors and ceiling, afraid of the third party to every conversation. They know that Germany is bound to be occupied, but their greatest fear is that the occupying troops will be the Russians, instead of the easy Americans. One belongs to the Nazi organizations because this is the utter essential of success in business, education, love or anything else. And one is completely saturated with Goebbels' lies, which have warped the German mind into shapeless obtuse monstrosity. The German people at home will never never believe what their SS, Gestapo and Wehrmacht have done in the occupied countries.

Now I am out again on the bright crowded shopping streets full of allied flags and the blown-up portraits of the reigning family. Our militiaman, who has been accompanying us, stops awkwardly and explains that he would like to leave now. He has seen someone up the street, a shady character who used to hang out around the Gestapo office. He'll let him go on for a while, then trail him from a distance. *Au revoir! Bonne chance!*

Chapter 8

The Chateau

After a week or so, we were on the move north again through the Ardennes forest, past the cross-roads towns of Bastogne and Visé, to the hamlet of Fouron St. Pierre, also known as St. Peters Voeren, just south of the border with the Dutch province of Limburg and a few miles from the German frontier. There were two sister villages, Fouron Le Comte and Fouron St. Martin. In this region the population spoke the language of the post-Charlemagne Middle Kingdom, a patois akin to that spoken in Luxembourg, neither German nor Flemish. The inhabitants were disparaging of the "Flamingands," who historically had sought to claim them as their own; they claimed to speak no Flemish (which was untrue) and used French as their second tongue. (The Fourons have continued to be a source of political contention in Belgium in the ensuing decades, claimed by both Flanders and French-speaking Wallonie.)

Today the area is a bedroom suburb of Liège, filled with a large number of housing developments. In 1944, it was a gently rolling Brueghel landscape of cultivated fields, stands of woodland, and clusters of brick farmhouses, marvelously quiet except for the faint distant sounds of artillery fire. Across the muddy road from the dominating chateau, the village consisted of an undistinguished little church and a small cluster of low brick buildings; one was a tavern whose interior decor and denizens seemed unchanged from the days of David Teniers.

The lives of the local peasantry were highly insulated; once when I was lost on a sunless day and asked for directions to Fouron St. Pierre, which could not have been more than a mile and a half away, I was told, *"Je ne sais pas, monsieur. Je ne suis pas du pays. Je suis de Fouron St. Martin, moi."* ["I don't know, mister. I'm not from these parts. I'm from Fouron St. Martin."] Like all of his countrymen, he wore wooden shoes, highly practical footwear since the unpaved roads were muddy quagmires after a rainfall. The outlook of these good folk was as primitive as their footwear. Arch Goldberg, a kindly ex-high school teacher from Connecticut, was asked by a teen-aged girl whether he was Catholic or Protestant; he replied that he was a Jew. She recoiled in horror and fright, with a curious look to see his horns.

Our home was the Chateau de la Commanderie of Fouron St. Pierre, a massive seventeenth-century structure that was already an architectural anachronism when it was constructed. It was surrounded by a moat and reached over a drawbridge and through a high gate, complete with portcullis. There were waterfowl in the moat, white doves soaring over the turrets, and a variety of fowl and beasts in the spacious courtyard, half-ringed with outbuildings. These housed the servants and a handful of farm workers, as well as an assortment of animals, carts, carriages, and assorted agricultural paraphernalia.

The outbuildings also became home to our guards, cooks, drivers, and other support personnel, while we privileged voice analysts set up our cots and our "fart sacks" (sleeping bags) in the main living room of the great house. On one wall was a splendid tapestry depicting the chateau as though it were a medieval castle, home to knights jousting in twelfth-century armor. To offset this fantasy, the room's centerpiece was a large dark table of baronial proportions. This was altogether appropriate, since the chateau's owner was an imposing noblewoman.

The "Royal Family"

November, 1944: In our old castle, the animals live practically in the same building as the human inhabitants and their dung is piled high outside the main entrance, giving a distinctive flavor to all the air we breathe. The rooms are gloomy, the plumbing is primitive. And yet for miles around here the castle is a symbol of wealth and power.

In a village five or six miles from here I talked to a woman who was proud because when she was a little girl her family had inhabited one of the buildings on the castle grounds, and she and her sister had been permitted by the Baroness to walk through the courtyard when they went to the village or to Church, whereas everyone else, until recently, always had to go around the back way, through the mud and ordure of the barnyard. I'll bet there isn't a man or woman in the area who, as a child, didn't like to sneak down to the great gates and peak into the courtyard for a sight of some grande dame or well-apparisoned noble youngster taking the air, or who didn't stand on the road at night and listen to the phonograph music wafted over the meadows, admire the handsome carriages clattering over the gravel paths, and see reflected on the moat the lights of the great room (where my bed, barracks bags, books and belongings now sprawl in disorder) in which fabulous, beautiful city-dwelling gentlemen and ladies danced, chatted and ate delicious bonbons like residents in the Never-Never lands of infantile story books. For a local subject of the Belgian crown (at present in the custody of A. Hitler) to question the Baroness's privileges is to counteract and destroy a myth deeply rooted in childhood experience. The salvation of Belgium and of Europe isn't going to come out of any feudal corner like the one in which I am tucked.

The baroness, who was always clad in an enveloping and shapeless black dress, suffered the presence of the American troops with even more resentful tolerance

The Chateau de la Commanderie at Fouron St. Pierre.

A mixed crew between shifts at the Chateau, 1944. The author is in the second row, fourth from the left.

than she had of the Germans who had cleared out shortly before our arrival. (They had used grenades to kill the fish in the moat.) As she periodically surveyed our temporary domain for signs of wear and tear, one could sense her calculating fresh items for the bill she would eventually submit to the authorities for reimbursement.

During our four-month stay, the baroness continued to occupy the family quarters on the second floor, along with the other members of what we called "The Royal Family," which included her niece, the countess (a pleasant-looking but heavy-set girl of eighteen or nineteen whose father, an Italian Air Force officer, had been captured in North Africa by the British) and a mysterious middle-aged companion, Mademoiselle Fifi, who appeared to be an unattached poor relation. I offered a retrospective comment on this establishment some months later:

March 28, 1945: For one who habitually considered Western Europe a center of political turmoil and universal enlightenment, compared with the U.S., [our stay in the chateau] was a revelation of the degree to which vicious feudal relics still determine the lives of millions of people and the affairs of nations. The "castle" in which we lived came out of a Viennese operetta, complete with moat, ceremonial gates, dowager Baroness, boar's head in the hallway, chickens in the courtyard, and a vast manure pile just outside the main entrance. Mme. La Baronne was a delightfully quaint old character with a cousin on Hitler's military staff. Her reaction, when an American bomber crashed in one of her numerous pine forests was a dismayed *"Ils ont écrasé les arbres!"* ["They've destroyed the trees!"]

Though in countless peasant homes in the locality, G.I.s had wrought all sorts of minor damages, one would always hear the inhabitants say, *"Ah que c'était bon quand ils étaient ici; nous avons eu de la peine de les voir partir."* [Oh, it was good when they were here. We were sorry to seem them leave."] On the other hand, the Baroness—who stole from us coal, coffee, and chocolate (she once ate part of a [paraffin] heating unit under the impression that it was a chocolate D-ration bar) and received free electricity, entertainment and a princely rent which the Belgian government will have to pay for under reverse lend-lease—the Baroness handed in a lengthy bill for damages (including those caused by enemy action) to her mouldy, crumbling old farmhouse.

What was amazing was that this eccentric old woman was still held in awe for miles around, and that she could speak to good respectable solid bourgeois citizens in the way that a medieval Baroness might speak to her serfs. While the people of the neighborhood were supposed to suffer through the winter on a rationed pailful of coal per capita (which they didn't get), the Baroness, despite her acres and acres of forest (which she sold at good prices for firewood) and the coal she stole from us, was able to secure an entire truckful of black-market coal, and no one was in a position to raise a word.

A frequent visitor to the chateau was an elderly baron, who arrived for dinner in a chauffeured motorcar (whose source of fuel was a subject of frequent discussion among us). Our officers had their billets somewhere in the same precincts, and socialized freely with the "Royals," who were treated to our generous food supplies. (It was commonly accepted among us that Gottlieb had explained to them that the difference between officers and enlisted men in the U.S. Army was roughly equivalent to that between aristocrats and peasants in Belgian society.)

At Home in the Chateau

Our senior non-coms occupied small rooms high up in the turret of the chateau. The comforts of this location were somewhat mitigated by its inaccessibility to either running water or toilet facilities. This was a particular inconvenience to Sergeant Axelrod, whose advancing age (he had by now already crossed the forty-year mark) required him to wake up occasionally from his slumbers. He kept a large tin can beside his bed and emptied it by moonlight through his battlement window, so that its contents splashed tinkle-tinkle into the moat in the middle of the night. The rest of us had to make our way on these errands through the courtyard, out through the gate, past the ever-present guard, and over to the outdoor latrine which had been set up for our use.

We took cold showers in an improvised stall in the courtyard and once or twice a week were taken on an hour-and-a-half-long truck ride to the dreary textile city of Verviers, where there was a hot-shower facility for troops coming in for rest from the field. Verviers otherwise had few attractions. During the Christ-

The center of Verviers in the 1920s.

mas season, Strotz and I visited the local department store, where St. Nicholas was handing out greeting cards to the youngsters, who whispered their wishes to him in traditional department-store style. Strotz insisted on taking his place in the queue, duly knelt down to receive the saint's blessing and received his card. As a lapsed Catholic this came quite naturally to him, while I found myself unable to rise (or rather kneel) to the occasion.

The long table in our living quarters was the center of our social life. I sat here reading Rabelais' *Gargantua et Pantagruel*, translating for my companions choice references to the practical use of a goose's long neck. Conversations were mostly carried on in a hush, since part of our crew, returned from or anticipating late-night duty, was always asleep or trying to sleep. Here occurred a great tragedy. One of our brethren had at great expense and with extraordinary resourcefulness obtained a precious bottle of Calvados brandy. He was about to share it when it slipped from his hands. Amid universal expressions of profound grief, the more desperate or enterprising of our group sought to salvage the liquid remains by slurping them up from the table or floor or sponging them up with handkerchiefs. These efforts were largely futile, and a cloud of gloom settled over us; the episode was talked about for days.

Our vehicles were always headed in different directions on miscellaneous supply errands, and on the main roads there was always enough military traffic to guarantee a lift. Sightseeing seems incongruous in wartime, but a limited number of destinations were within reach on my free days. To the north, Holland remained under German occupation, except for the odd-shaped province of Limburg. Its capital, Maastricht, was notable for its two Gothic cathedrals, one of which had been converted into a Reformed church.

At an outdoor hospitality center where a group of women were serving coffee to soldiers, I fell into conversation with a plump, cheerful-looking Jewish lady who had somehow survived the occupation. From her purse she took out a sheaf of snapshots of her daughter and other family members who had been sent to "the East." She had not heard from them and wanted my assurance that they were all right, although both she and I knew perfectly well what had happened to them. It was a difficult moment.

In Maastricht, in a small rococo jewel of a theater, I went one evening to a performance of "The Barretts of Wimpole Street," starring the great Katherine Cornell. The rapt and enthusiastic audience was dominated by infantrymen sent back from the front lines for a brief period of "R and R" (rest and relaxation). Our rifles and steel helmets occasionally clattered to the floor, punctuating the play with reminders of the present.

To the east, across another border, was Aachen, the first and only German city to be taken when our armies swept through France and Belgium in August. The front line lay just on its other side, and the scene was permeated by the sound of machine-gun fire and the scent of death. Only a few residents remained. The apartments of the others had been ransacked. The cathedral that housed the remains of Charlemagne had been damaged by artillery fire. A dead horse lay for weeks on one of the main streets. Someone had sliced a chunk of steak off one hindquarter. Nearby, on the brick side of a destroyed building, a large painted advertisement depicted a happy housewife smiling at a basket of laundry. The headline read, *"Persilgepflegt musst Wäsche sein!"* [Laundry must be cared for with Persil!].

Our mess sergeant could not stand our behind-the-lines inactivity. Every once in a while, seeking action, he would head for Aachen and the battleground, muttering, "I'm going to get me some krauts!" He always returned safely, but without any human ears or other trophies of his marksmanship.

October, 1944: Deeper than the purely intellectual knowledge of these things which we culled from periodicals back in the States, one must see for oneself the blitzed schoolhouse, the looted synagogue, the wilted young widows, the hands maimed by the Gestapo, talk to deserters from the Wehrmacht, to prison guards returned to liberated territory from Frankfurt on Sept. 12 ("Yes, the Germans hate the SS, but their minds are rotten, they believe the old Nazi lies") and be fed hot soup by farmers saved by the American advance from shooting as hostages.

November, 1944: Belgium has now introduced conscription for certain age categories of young men, some of whom go to England for training and some to France. *Gendarmes* and frontier guards are not permitted to be stationed in the region from which they come. If an official in a district with Flemish as its official language gets a letter in French he must answer it in Flemish. If he answers in French he can be fired.

On Armistice Day, November 11, 1944, the local civilian officials asked us to send an honor guard to a nearby cemetery for the dead of the First World War. I was part of the squad assembled to deliver a military salute on this occasion, for which a small group of dignitaries, relatives, and curious neighbors had assembled. We pretended to put on our most professional military bearing and Sergeant Axelrod directed us to ready, aim, and fire at the sky. The shots rang out in chaotic succession rather than in unison. Along with several other members of the squad, I made the mistake of pressing the release lever on my carbine's bullet clip instead of the safety catch, and had to scramble for the clip when I should have been doing a right face and marching away. Thus are battles lost!

There was new word from friends at home:

November 15, 1944: So Oscar is out of the Army! Strangely enough—you may think—I don't envy him. It's not merely the vast store of new experiences I've been accumulating that makes me say this, but the simple fact that I wouldn't feel right if I were anywhere but where I am (well, in general. I could think of more lively and interesting places to be now than in this old chateau!).

November 24, 1944: Yesterday brought us the Army's usual sumptuous Thanksgiving dinner, with all the turkey we could eat, stuffing, mashed potatoes, peas and corn, celery, cranberry sauce, hot biscuits, pumpkin pie and candy. It was a vivid contrast to some of the less tasteful stews we've been getting all too often. Last night I was at the home of some farmers in the neighborhood. I enjoy the pleasure of eating out of plates instead of from my mess kit. The only trouble is that some of the old people speak no French—nothing in fact but their own local patois. Each village has its own dialect, and these are often so different from each other that the residents of one community can't understand the residents of another only 4 or 5 miles down the road. It's amazing to realize that people will spend their whole lives in one little hamlet and consider it a great excursion when they visit a town that is only a few miles away.

The Commanding Officer

I profiled Ferdinand (Fred) Gottlieb, our commanding officer, in a paper for a graduate course in social anthropology that I took in the summer of 1946 after leaving the army. My recollections of him were still very fresh:

Gottlieb minimized his personal contacts with the support personnel, leaving censure and punishment to his adjutant whenever possible. Regardless of their behavior he was unwilling to institute court-martial proceedings, on the theory that "I want every man should have a clean record when he goes out of here."

He recognized his educational inferiority to the linguists, many of whom were older than he, and was extremely uncomfortable with them. He disguised this by spreading good cheer as he walked about, smiling widely and stopping to ask each man by name, "How's it going today?" [He had a fresh good-looking little-boy's face, but his smile was lopsided.] When his goals of perfection were not reached he felt his own achievement marred and reacted with appropriate intensity. A scratch on a truck fender was a knife thrust in his own heart. If a carbine was dirty, if the men marched poorly, this was an insult to his ideals, and he vented his chagrin in an intemperate outburst at the offenders. "Why don't you watch where you going with my truck? Are you blind or something?" (He employed the personal possessive freely in speaking of the organization, its equipment and its men.)

This volatility and emotionalism aroused intense antagonism among his subordinates. He was aware of this, and after each display would retire into quiet obscurity and become excessively cordial and solicitous. He bore few lengthy grudges, and was always surprised and hurt to find an individual harboring continuing resentment because of a single encounter.

His temper was not always expressed privately. He delighted in calling formations and delivering little speeches inveighing against the faults he had observed. "Phallus [fellows], this area's been looking goddamn lousy. There is going to be no liberty run tonight nor tomorrow night if this area ain't cleaned up, and I mean cleaned up!" But sometimes his speeches were occasioned by feelings of optimism and enthusiasm. "By us everything is democratic," he said once, and when a change of location was planned, or if he had picked up a particularly choice rumor of general interest, he would call a meeting and smile and happily tell everyone about it.

When he first announced the move to the Chateau, Gottlieb waxed enthusiastic. "I want everything should be kept clean, and we have a mat outside so everybody wipes his feet before he goes in. Honest, it's too good for us. It's like putting pigs in a palace."

Gottlieb took to sleeping late in the mornings, often until noon, and amused himself by taking frequent "business" trips in his jeep. The work was carried on competently without him. He would appear at the operational site, "inspect" the vans and show vigorous anger over minor imperfections he observed—a dirty floor, an undeciphered message, a man eating a candy bar or reading a book. "Suppose the General walks in. Then he blames *me*!" [Eisenhower did come visiting one day, but with plenty of advance warning. In the operations van, Gottlieb pointed to Strotz and several others and announced, with what Strotz took to be a patronizing air, "These are some of our research boys."]

With persistently decreasing frequency, Gottlieb also served as duty officer, a task that required his presence during a six-hour shift. During extremely busy periods, he became tense and excitable and excessively demanding of his subordinates. His authoritative, decisive attitudes were, however, an asset in the larger military aspects of his work. He never failed to give an opinion if one was called for, and did so definitively and dogmatically, even when his judgments were based on pure fancy. Since the role of duty officer required this type of sharp, quick reaction, he performed it impressively. Even on the job he strove to fulfill the Hollywood conception of an officer; on the telephone his speech was strangely flavored with expressions like "Righ-ight!" and "Roger-Dodger," which seemed to derive more from the vocabulary of the movies than from current army usage.

When operations were slow, Gottlieb fidgeted. Not accustomed to sustained reading, he picked up papers and laid them down again or elaborately cleaned his fingernails. He made a ritual of the daily test of the radio transmitter, taking a child's pleasure in the microphone. The non-commissioned officers who served as his assistants dreaded his appearances, for he found it continually necessary to give orders: "Stop scratching on that pad!" "Don't shuffle your feet!" He invented new duties and procedures and forgot about them as quickly as they were assigned. Increasingly he shifted his duties to more competent enlisted personnel.

He took a peculiar delight in captured German materials—Nazi flags, pictures of Hitler, anti-Semitic literature—and gleefully spoke of decorating the austerely functional interiors of the vans with them. (Hanging up a scarlet swastika banner: "It's not for operations, phallus, but it looks good!") A large colored print of an evil Jew menacing Europe aroused his particular delight. If eyebrows were raised he laughed and said, "Don't take me serious!"

The isolated and secret character of Flap Dog made Gottlieb relatively impervious to supervision. The work of the organization was highly respected in higher headquarters and he was assumed to be responsible for its success. Superior officers [though (as he told me after the war) not the Squadron commander, Maj. Theodore Silverstein, in civilian life a professor of medieval English literature at the University of Chicago] considered him energetic and capable. In their presence he invariably became very boyish and affable, agreeing with their opinions and showing all possible respect. Inspecting generals and colonels were always impressed by the complex and mysterious nature of Flap Dog's equipment and activities and by Gottlieb's informed behavior as he showed them around. (With a sweet smile: "I'm sorry I can't say any more, Colonel. That's all top secret information.") He put his Motor Section to furious work repairing a captured German vehicle, which he ceremoniously presented to a high-ranking superior.

In his zeal to make the Detachment "perfect" Gottlieb would quite fearlessly go to higher channels to get things done for his men. If a conflict developed with another unit, he introduced authority: "I tell my general."

In his relations with the other officers in our unit, Gottlieb was spectacularly less successful. There were four other officers subordinate to him, all first lieutenants like himself. One was in continual conflict with him and was finally sent away at his own request. The others accepted Gottlieb's domination for the simple reason that they were in a pleasant safe position and were unwilling to take the risk of transfer to a replacement depot. Their attitudes ranged from cowering subservience to grudging toleration. The officers were billeted in the same large room and were together for meals and social activity. With his characteristic impetuosity and changeability of mood, Gottlieb turned military discipline on and off according to his fancy. If he was in good humor he wished to be treated as a pal, but if something went wrong he became the Detachment commander, and used his tongue without fear of rebuttal. In the evening the officers not on duty played cards, drank and censored the enlisted men's mail, a major pastime. Interesting letters were read aloud for the edification of the others. Since this was known to the men, their mail was especially ripe with gripes.

Gottlieb's attitude toward the average Frenchman or Belgian was one of unveiled contempt. "These Frogs are only out to rob you. Look what kinds of houses they live in, without toilets! How you going to teach these people anything?"

The officers ate butter, the enlisted men oleomargarine. The officers were served at table from plates. The enlisted men waited on line and ate from mess kits. "We got to have discipline, phallus," Gottlieb told a formation. "I didn't make these rules. It's the Army. After the War, I meet you on the street, we shake hands, I go in with you and buy you a beer. But now we're in the Army, we got to have discipline, we got to have military courtesy." Saluting was compulsory within the chateau's courtyard. The one accessible toilet in the building was reserved for daytime use by the officers, while the men used a crude outdoor latrine beyond the gate. While the enlisted men and other officers wore battle dress, Gottlieb was always immaculate with tie, highly polished boots and Eisenhower jacket with bright insignia.

When we moved into Germany Gottlieb showed the same solicitude for property that he had had for the Baroness's lawn and fir trees. "We got to make these people feel we're their friends," he sometimes declared, as in a famous effort to keep a group of American infantrymen from slaughtering a cow for their dinner. Scornfully he contrasted the ragged appearance of the Russian and Polish Displaced Persons with those of the clean and well-fed Germans.

Shortly before the end of the war, Gottlieb was awarded the Bronze Star, and then his captaincy.

Strotz's German was less than perfect, and instead of monitoring the airwaves with the rest of us he was placed in the operations van, where he coordinated our reports of Luftwaffe activity with the direction-finding results and other available intelligence. He did this far better than any of the officers, and stood in for Gottlieb much of the time. Strotz detested all the trappings of the military. When he received the Bronze Star (on Gottlieb's recommendation), he threw the medal into the fireplace, and resisted my efforts to retrieve it from the flames. Fifteen years later, when he was already a distinguished economist (eventually he was president and chancellor of Northwestern University) I mentioned to him that I had come across traces of Gottlieb, who had become a practicing architect in a New York suburb. Strotz immediately tracked down Gottlieb's phone number and called him: "Gottlieb? This is Shtrotz (Gottlieb had always given the name a Berlin pronunciation), from Flap Dog. Remember me? Go fuck yourself!"

A Trip to Dinant

November 28, 1944: With 17 men in a room and only one table to read or write at, there's always at least one chap with nothing to do except talk who keeps the others from their books and letter-writing.

I had a V-mail letter from Oscar asking me to look up the sister of Mrs. Chermayeff who lives in a town some distance from here. Her family haven't heard from her since the war began.

December 2, 1944: I spent the whole day today hitchhiking across Belgium to find the sister of Mrs. Chermayeff, whom I found all right.

The road to Dinant followed the east bank of the Meuse River; when I arrived I discovered that the main part of the city lay on the opposite shore. The high suspension bridge had been destroyed and was in the process of being rebuilt by a company of engineers. Like riggers on the skeleton of a skyscraper, they were crossing back and forth on the six-inch-wide steel beams that were to hold the roadway. Having come all this way, I had to swallow my anxiety. I crossed with slow and deliberate steps, fearful of being unbalanced by my heavy steel helmet and my carbine, trying to keep my mind off the river far below. It was only when I set out on my return trip that I was made aware of a ferry shuttling back and forth between the two river banks.

Almost a month later, during the Battle of the Bulge, Dinant became a direct objective of the German army, prompting me to reflect further about my visit.[1]

December 27, 1944: A kilometer is psychologically longer than a mile at home. This latest and last [German] offensive threatens the welfare of Mrs. Chermayeff's sister and her Belgian husband (she sculptress, he painter), stranded in Dinant. She had been jailed by the Nazis for 9 months *pendant l'Occupation* for putting flowers on a British war memorial, and before they pulled out she and her husband had been sought as hostages. I worry about them not because they are any more important than any of the thousands of people who fearfully wait for the return of the Panzers [the dreaded German "Panther" tanks] as old men wait for death—but because they happen to fit into my consciousness as individuals, with relations, yearnings and despair for the future. ("Tell me, do you think there will be opportunities for an artist in America after the War? A man I know, a painter, went to America, but the only work he could get was to paint ceilings and walls, except for one rich man who wanted his portrait on a plate.")

The Battle of the Bulge

Winter snows arrived early in 1944. The difficult country roads became even more difficult, as our four-wheel-drive vehicles slithered and spun their wheels. With the start of the von Rundstedt offensive on December 16, our hitherto routine operations took a new turn. The Luftwaffe's bombers emerged from a period of hibernation, flying close to the ground to avoid detection. One passed over our heavily camouflaged field installation, prompting some futile carbine fire in its general direction. Inside the vans, our radios crackled constantly with testimony to raging air battles. Rumors abounded of incursions by English-speaking German paratroopers masquerading as G.I.s. The sounds of anti-aircraft fire filled the night. We heard talk of SS units who murdered their prisoners.

The First Army to our south had been hit hard. One night the men of our sister unit, Flap Charlie, arrived at our chateau in just a handful of their vehicles. They had been forced to abandon their intelligence vans and other equipment to escape the oncoming Wehrmacht. From then on, through the entire Battle of the Bulge, our detachment had to serve as the ears of the 9th Tactical Air Command as well as of the 19th TAC and the 8th Air Force bomber command in England. We doubled our guard and turned away visitors, including the old baron, who showed up for his usual dinner despite the confusion. *"Vous faites votre devoir,"* ("You are doing your duty,") he told me with true *noblesse oblige*.

December 19, 1944: We've got a Christmas tree in our front hallway, all decorated with color paper ornaments. Everyone sits around the table, plays solitaire and wonders what to write about.

December 25, 1944: The people in whose chateau we're billeted treated us to cider and pies this noon—also little tarts with whipped cream on top (the first whipped cream I've had in the E.T.O. At night there was beer and cognac drunk in the sanctity of our chamber, and my friend Pierre [Magermans, who with his wife Elise ran the local school] had brought over a box of waffles today as a Christmas present.

December, 1944: M. Magermans père [Pierre's father] had been married only three months when Germany invaded Belgium during the last war. For five years, as a Belgian soldier, he was far from home while his wife and baby son remained under German occupation. The only communication consisted of occasional letters forwarded via relatives in Holland. (I have glanced at some of the faded letters he wrote from the front. They are lonely and tender and begin, "My dear little Marie.") It is hard, looking at this solid elderly person and his good wife to realize that their comfortable home and their family were built out of five years of agonized waiting and frustration. What can I reasonably complain about?

Late one evening, the activity in our vicinity heated up. All of us were summoned to our battle stations; mine were above one of the livestock buildings at an open window in the farmer's apartment. We waited apprehensively, while the family cowered in another part of their humble quarters. Planes roared overhead. Suddenly we heard a shot, then others. Someone had spotted a parachute. The paratrooper attack had begun. We fired into the darkness at targets that failed to materialize. Gottlieb frantically called for reinforcements, and after a long interval, a solitary Sherman tank arrived and took an exposed position outside the main entrance, where paratroopers might have made short work of it. There were no paratroopers, only the pilot of a German fighter plane who had parachuted after it was hit by anti-aircraft fire. He had broken his ankle, was caught by some civilians, and turned over to Gottlieb, who tended to him solicitously and sent him off to the hospital. We all eventually went back to our routines. Despite all the noise, Klaus, a big sad-looking German refugee, had slept peacefully through the entire episode.

Some days later the weather cleared, the siege of Bastogne was lifted, Patton's Third Army began a pincer operation, and the earlier front was more or less restored. We were thrilled as huge formations of our bombers soared overhead again. The Baroness watched them unsmilingly; her sympathies lay with those about to be bombarded. *"Et les pauvres gens là bas?"* ("And those poor people over there?")

Return to Paris

There was another trip to Paris, this time with a mission. Lt. Roland Given (the Norwegian speaker) had once found a miracle cure for his encroaching baldness, a balm called *Pétrole Hahn*. I was instructed to find it at any cost, but a massive search of pharmacies was altogether unsuccessful.

January 30, 1945: I've been to Paris on pass—a day and a half travel each way (by truck)—2 days in the big city, stopovers in Soissons and Reims. It's good to get back to civilization for a while, even though one forgets oneself at times. I walked into an Army office in Paris [actually a hotel on the Champs Elysées]—velvety rugs on the floors, polished mahogany furniture, officers with gorgeously pressed uniforms and sparkling brass, and asked the M.P. on guard where the "latrine" was. [He looked at me disdainfully before directing me to "the men's room."]

Paris, despite uniforms, fuel and food shortages and other wartime restrictions, preserves an almost peacetime aspect compared to the battered towns of Belgium and Germany. It reminded me more of New York than even London did, particularly in the crowded subway. I saw Verdi's "Otello" at the Opera, three one act plays at the Théatre des Mathurins, and even the old Marx Brothers film "A Night at the Opera" with dubbed-in French sound that made it even more hilarious than ever. The Louvre was mostly closed up, with everything removed for the duration except the ancient Greek, Roman and Assyrian statuary. Prices in Paris are terrific, particularly for us soldiers, because the rate of exchange (50 francs = $1) is so unfair. I spent some time in the big department stores, Au Printemps and Galeries Lafayette. Almost the entire first floors are devoted to the sale of beauty preparations of one sort or another.

An advertisement in the newly reappeared Paris edition of the *Herald Tribune:*

>American Soldier!
>In France, Carter's Little Liver Pills are Known as
>Les Petites Pillules Carter Pour Le Foix!

In late February of 1945 a new Allied offensive began in the valley of the Roer River, and we headed off into the German Rhineland.

Chapter 9

The Discovery of Germany

A letter from my father reported that he had received word that his old mother in Odessa had been murdered by the Nazis. I wrote back from a small German town where we had temporarily set up quarters.

March 12, 1945: Daddy darling, I only hope that I may always be as good a son to you and Mom as you have always been to your mother. I am not at all thinking now of what circumstances did or did not permit you to do for her in any material sense, but rather of the deep love you felt for her and the degree to which you were successful in making her aware of it. I cannot think of any more appropriate time to express this thought, which never leaves my consciousness: the honor and affection in which I hold my parents do not exist simply because you are my parents but because you are good people.

It did not take the episode of which you have written me to put my sense of the issues in this war on a vivid and personal level. But the shock of your letters came at a good time in terms of activating emotions that are called for by my present situation. I do not believe in bashing German civilians over the head indiscriminately or in wantonly destroying whatever German property the war has so far left untouched. I don't think one can engage in such personal acts without debasing one's own morality in the process. But there are other and more effective ways of expressing one's own implacable hostility, and these I intend to use. It is a difficult task to extend a theoretical hatred to specific individuals who have done you no immediate personal harm and who look and react just like people one knows. But I intend to retain and to *live* my memories, not merely of atrocities spoken of or read of in books but of things I have seen.

It is only just, though nonetheless horrible, that Germany is now feeling in full measure the fury of destruction which she brought to the rest of Europe. Since I am more than 25 miles away from it, censorship regulations permit me to mention Aachen, which I have been in a number of times. Though it is by no means the worst destroyed town I have seen in ruins, it is by far the largest. I cannot decide in my own mind whether to wish that destruction of the Aachen type be visited on the whole of Germany in partial punishment for its crimes or that as much as possible of Germany's great productive capacity be spared to furnish restitution to those of her victims who still remain alive.

Ruin and Rubble

March, 1945: Of all the ruin and destruction I have seen in Europe I think that Germany has received the largest share. I had been in Aachen a number of times over a period of four or five months, and had found a degree of destruction almost as bad as St. Lo (except on a vastly larger scale), but it had never occurred to me that Aachen might simply be an introduction to the other German cities I was to see.[1] I have been in a number of others, and merely in them have already seen more devastation than I had previously observed in all the rest of Europe. The significant thing is that almost all the damage to be found in the towns we see has been done in the course of the war by aerial bombardment. I am therefore led to expect that as we continue to advance deeper into Germany we shall find the pattern repeated constantly.

The fact that the bombing has of course concentrated on military or industrial targets makes for a patchwork crazy quilt of contrasts. One may walk through towns or urban areas which, except for the white flags fluttering from the windows, seem as remote from war as any similar blocks in Brooklyn, N.Y., or Nashville, Tennessee. And yet there are other areas that are gutted, smashed and desolate; on the skeleton walls there hangs a mocking dentist's plaque, a druggist's shingle. The efficient Germans have stacked the rubble along the sidewalks in neat piles.

Almost every bombed building carries a Nazi slogan, glaring in large whitewashed letters: "We will never surrender!" "First work, then victory!" "The soldiers rely on us!" "Just now really, Heil Hitler!" "It's up to you!" "For the Führer, your trust and duty!" "Even in the last free minute, work can help for victory!" Yellowing posters proclaim the Gauleiter's requisition of motor transport, the Führer's establishment of the Volkssturm, Dr. Goebbels' version of the Yalta Conference entitled, "Stalin's proclamation to the German people"[2] (Sample: "A Russian PW reports that Stalin has ordered the Red Army that when it takes Berlin the entire population is to be massacred, except for the blonde-haired maidens, who are to be thrown to the lust of the Bolshevist bandits".[3]).

Our only answer to this Nazi propaganda, incidentally, has been to post prominently in public places dull official AMG [Allied Military Government] documents in fine print, dealing with such subjects as the color and size in millimeters of the new occupation currency and the points of registration for new ration cards. An Army-sponsored German newspaper has been issued sporadically in Aachen for some time, but its circulation in more recently occupied areas is late and negligible.

The OWI [Office of War Information], or whoever is responsible, has really missed the boat on a great opportunity, to influence the thinking of the hundreds of thousands of Germans in the areas we control. Many of them are older people who have been subjected to other influences than Nazism during their lives; all of them have just undergone crushing and exciting events that leave them groping for new perspectives. If we are unable to supply or at least suggest the truth to them at this time, when attitudes are still molten and chaotic, then unquestionably the tendency for most Germans will be to fall back on the only ideology they have to hand, the Nazi one. And these people, particularly since electricity has in many places not yet been restored and radios are not operating, are hungry for news and information. Since they are human beings I would imagine that a good proportion of them are also hungry for ideas.

What a tremendous effect a small selection of clever, bitter, anti-Nazi posters could have, for example, among people who have suffered greatly from the war but do not always have the intellectuality or imagination to link the war's evils with Fascism's evils. But nothing along these lines has been done as far as I know and I suspect that nothing will be done.

In spite of all the wreckage one sees here no matter where one looks, it is impossible to avoid remarking that this is a rich and modern country. The Germans have lived surprisingly well these last few years, and small wonder! They have stolen all the wealth of Europe to keep themselves comfortable. There are many striking contrasts with Belgium; it is unreal and disconcerting to see such well dressed, neat-looking people with starched white collars, pressed pants and briefcases walking through streets that are merely defiles through mountains of bricks and junk and rubble. How in the hell did they ever manage to get so spruced up?

Just as one might expect, the villages too are neat and solid, without the familiar manure piles stacked against the kitchen doors. One thing in particular that strikes me about Germany, as compared with the rest of Western Europe, is the enormous number of young children. It is one thing to accept the vague generalization that the Nazi plan for world domination called for a weakening of the subject peoples and a converse boosting of the German birth rate, and another thing to see the reality in human terms. The Germans kept the French and Belgian PWs under lock and key; the French and Belgian children are few and puny. But the Wehrmacht sent its own soldiers home regularly on stud furloughs, and encouraged its unmarried members to let their seed fall where it might for the glory of Führer and Fatherland. The result is that a great proportion of the remaining population consists of healthy-looking blond youngsters. The little boys all wear their Hitler Youth caps (cut like the army caps, but black, and without insignia), probably because they don't have any other kind.

Except for these notable particulars it is difficult at a superficial glance to descry the mark of Fascism on the outward appearance of Germany. As I may have observed in the letter I wrote about my first trip to Aachen, it would make things a lot easier if the Germans had all grown horns and turned blue in the last twelve years. The trouble is that they look just like Americans, Frenchmen, Hollanders, Belgians or Luxembourgeois, and that as one sees them in their personal lives one is forced, however unwillingly, to recognize that they laugh and worry and love and suffer and gossip in ways that are too deeply rooted in Western man for ideologies to alter.

It is difficult to stifle compassion for an old woman rummaging in the remains of her bombed house, or to resist the appeal of a four year old boy to whom uniforms are all alike and who waves and laughs and cries *"Soldaten, Soldaten!"* as one walks by. It is difficult to return nods of greeting with stony stares. For most G.I.s these things are not merely difficult but impossible; kids ask for chocolate, chewing gum, and even cigarettes just as kids do wherever our army goes; infantrymen, including occasional blithe spirits wearing "liberated" tall silk hats and morning coats, cannot suppress their normal male-animal yawps when their open trucks pass pretty girls on the road. (On this subject I think that the almost complete success of the non-fraternization policy has been immeasurably aided by the low and doggy condition of German female pulchritude.)

This veneer of characteristically human value and human virtue somehow manages to coexist with all the unspeakable vileness that is Fascism. Go into the houses of these innocent-looking little bourgeois and you will find the inevitable party membership books, the pictures of Hitler, the certificates of service to the H.J. [Hitler Youth], the monstrous, murderous Nazi classics, the photo of son Hans who is with the Waffen-SS on the Eastern Front. I vividly recall reading that one of the Nazi executioners tried by the Russians for his work at a murder camp in Poland, where he put thousands of victims to horrible death, very proudly displayed to investigators snapshots of his wife and two small children. That epitomizes the whole dilemma.

Or this: I was standing on the street the other day near a block of buildings which temporarily served as a displaced persons center for Russian and Polish ex-slaves awaiting repatriation. A German woman came up to me, followed by an anxious looking little man, and complained that the Russians had taken the little man's bicycle away from him. I shrugged my shoulders and pretended not to understand but I wanted to rage and fume and scream; "They have taken your bicycle; you have taken their lives." But I'm sure the woman would never have realized what that might mean; the great crime was accomplished through official channels and with legal papers and rubber stamps,—it was therefore no crime but a positive good,—the little crime was circumstantial and personal and therefore dastardly.

I have seen how these slave laborers, civilians and war prisoners alike, were kept in wretched barracks on the grounds of the factories in which they worked, with barbed wire and sentinels. They were fed rotten cabbages and flogged like animals; they were required to wear blue patches bearing the letters "OST" (East), but their shabby clothing was enough to identify them.

(Digression: Just to see the way Ukrainian peasants wear Western clothes is to strike at one of the miracles of the Russian Revolution. In a matter of twenty-five years a people living by medieval folkways is forced to adjust itself to a modern framework of social customs, and the weird contradictions resulting can be sensed in the sight of a stocky broadfaced, grinning fellow, with a felt hat backwards stuck way back on his head, wearing a sleeveless, collarless white shirt, with a jacket draped carelessly over one shoulder like a toga. Just like movie Russians, these chaps at a moment's notice will whip out an accordion and start a graceful sensuous dance that ends up as a *kazatsky* [traditional squatting dance],smiling like angelic babies or croaking the words to the tune. One chap wore a sporty jacket and a violent red tie, oh yes, and a Tyroler hat. But he had a beautiful pair of long thin red mustachios elaborately curled several times at each end.)

The Germans tried to break their spirit, they said, but they couldn't, not even when they machine-gunned numerous Russian war prisoners at the time of their retreat across the Rhine. I wondered whether during their stay in Germany they [the Russians] had met any "good Germans" and they said that yes, in the factories there had been a small number of "Thälmanns," "Communists."[4] The activity of these people, however, seems to have been entirely unpolitical,—they would smuggle food or cigarettes to the foreign laborers, and otherwise indicate their sympathies, but actual revolutionary effort must have been almost nonexistent and this accords well with what I heard in Luxembourg. (Incidentally, about a month and a half ago Strotz returned to visit his relatives there and found that their village had been the scene of a battle during the German offensive and that one of the homes we had visited had been destroyed.[5])

Perhaps what I have written earlier above has not quite conveyed the picture of the Germans' attitude toward us. It has been overwhelmingly hostile, but also surprisingly unmilitant. Perhaps as we penetrate deeper into the core of the Reich, where greater numbers of able-bodied men will be found in the areas behind our lines, we shall begin to meet something of the kind of guerrilla opposition which so confounded the Nazis in the countries they occupied. Thus far, I know personally of no "incidents," though of course there are occasional reports of such in the *Stars and Stripes*. I have seen no provoking gestures, though there is hate in many of the faces that I see and a dismal deathly apathy in most.

One thing which has somewhat surprised me is that I have noted none of the excessive meekness which one might reasonably expect as the reaction to the shattered superman myth. The only episode which indicates the existence of any actively anti-Nazi feeling happened several weeks ago. I was standing with a friend reading a Nazi poster in a nearby city. A middle-aged couple that was passing stopped. The woman pointed to the poster, read a line sarcastically and began to laugh falsely, almost hysterically. It was as though she were desperately trying to show us two American soldiers that there were Germans who were disillusioned in a critical as well as in a passive sense.

My conclusions are undoubtedly quite clear already. My appreciation of the complexity of the post-war European problem has immeasurably grown. In many ways our treatment of the conquered Germans has already been too humane, as a Dutch soldier with his family in occupied Holland remarked to me grimly. Yet within certain limits we will never avoid being humane, unless we descend to the Nazi level. When I think of an inhumane act on our part toward the Germans I think, not of population transfers, reparations to the plundered countries, export of conscripted German labor or detention of German PWs abroad in a conscious policy of reducing the German birth rate. I think rather of the possibility, proposed by some, of mass executions, or of the proposed wanton destruction of German productive power.

March 28, 1945: As for Germany: I don't believe that my feelings have undergone any change since I came here (if anything they have been strengthened by the horror stories told by liberated slave laborers and by the recent news of my old grandmother's murder) but I have certainly acquired a new appreciation for the degree to which the German national character is still in a dynamic state. Human beings are uncannily complex, even after twelve years of Fascism, it seems. It has been of terrific impact to see the degree to which Germany has been destroyed. I have been in Köln [Cologne], Aachen and a number of other cities, and the unfailing repetition of the same pattern of ruin makes me wonder whether any part of Germany we come to will be significantly different. I am not one of those who rejoices in any destruction of German productive capacity, because I think that the French and Poles and Russians and Dutch will have to suffer along with the Germans, who should be made to suffer in other than merely material ways. The most important job we have to accomplish is to give the Germans a sense of guilt. I fear that most of those we've conquered don't have a bit of it, and that is the best proof that Goebbels has done his job well.

Inside the Third Reich

Our activities heated up again in the last few months of the war when the Luftwaffe brought out its new jet fighters, which could fly rings around our Mustangs and began to take a heavy toll of our heavy, slow bombers. Although their remaining airport runways were now heavily cratered, the Germans had kept their well-camouflaged aircraft in forests adjacent to their superb Autobahnen, which they used successfully to take off and land.

I finally had the opportunity to put my earlier training in cryptanalysis to work. The Luftwaffe used a standard map of Europe, divided into quadrants designated by letter and number. The letters were identified by easily recognized names that reduced confusion amidst the crackle of the air waves, just like the American military's use of Able, Baker, Charlie instead of ABC. Thus when a Luftwaffe controller spoke of activity at Hanni Nordpol (HN) 4, we could locate it at the same moment as the fighters he was trying to alert. We were thrown into confusion when the Germans suddenly dropped the letter code that they had used throughout the war and began using the names of cities instead. Unlike the letter code, the initial letter of the city code appeared to have no relation to the geographic coordinates. My solution was to chart what the direction-finding equipment had indicated as the originating location of each message and relate this to the city names in the text. My immediate superior, a taciturn emigré staff sergeant from Los Angeles named Bob Spiegel, insisted on signing the memorandum in which I explained this before he relayed it to higher headquarters. By this time, however, the war was winding down and Luftwaffe action was sporadic.

April 1, 1945: I know it's Easter because I rode for many miles through Germany this afternoon, and everywhere, in all the towns and villages, the people were dressed up in holiday clothes and out strolling. How prosperous they look, these Germans! Their clothes are so new and well cut, their faces so full and well fed compared to those of the other peoples whom I have seen in Europe. One would never think, as one rides through many a solid, clean, and untouched hamlet, that this country has gone through almost six years of "total" war.

Yet always one finds startling juxtapositions of serenity and chaos. On a block of bombed and gutted buildings one may often find a single house quite intact, with new glass in the windows, curtains, flowerpots and a doormat indicating habitation. At one point, the road may pass through a village without even a bullet mark on any of its walls; half a mile away a blasted field of rubble is the remnant of its neighbor. (I have seen blasted homes, schools, churches and hospitals in all the countries of the Old World so far, but a shelled cemetery—it was adjacent to a road junction—was a new and unpleasant sight. Nothing startling; no skeleton limbs protruding from broken coffins; just the usual shell holes with tombstones scattered in and about them, and a few weary women looking for the visible remnants of their previous lives.) Although many or most of the factories one sees have been pounded into mounds of brick, with the ubiquitous fingers of the chimneys still standing, one frequently passes great mills, quite uncamouflaged and yet quite undamaged, which must have been in full production right up to the time of their capture.

I wonder and wonder these days about what happens next to the German economy. Just now there isn't any, of course, in the territory we take. The farmers simply continue to work the land, which now means not merely ploughing and sowing and the other ordinary chores, but in many cases filling in extensive rows of trenches, foxholes, and anti-tank ditches. That is a bigger job than it may sound like and one that can only be done through some sort of cooperative effort. The German farmers haven't fared badly in general, compared to the farmers of formerly occupied Europe, who were looted of their livestock, particularly of their horses. (The Wehrmacht is in considerable part horse-drawn, and now even baby-carriage-drawn, according to the reports Strotz heard in Luxembourg.)

The small tradesmen, of whom there remain very few, may also continue at their jobs without any especially dramatic readjustment. Rather few of the food shops are open, and the queues outside them are long. Minor municipal employees, those engaged in certain public utilities, for instance, also continue to function. A growing number of people are employed by military government for various purposes: clearing rubble, repairing roads and other menial jobs, none of any military significance. (I took a shower a few weeks ago at what had been the public bathhouse of a German city. It was taken over by the Army, but the haggard old woman who guarded the bathrooms, and the little bristly haired man who worked in the shower-room and squeegeed the water down the drains continued their duties as always). Nonetheless this covers only a limited proportion of the entire productive population. In the city streets of a weekday morning one can see hundreds of well-dressed gentlemen scurrying about with briefcases under their arms, and one can't help puzzling over what's in those briefcases. One can't help puzzling either over how all the millions of conquered Germans who are neither farmers nor grocers nor streetcleaners get the money to buy the food to keep alive.

German industry is either annihilated or altogether disorganized. It will have to remain disorganized for the time being, unless we decide that punishment of war criminals ends with execution of Hitler and a few well-chosen leaders of the SS. Only complete and total planning, coupled with complete socialization (for European rather than for German social ends), can rebuild the destroyed economy whose corporate ownership has been completely involved in the murderous corruption of the Nazi State. This is brought home to me all the more forcefully by the sight of countless cold factory chimneys, of precious machinery thickly rusting in roofless buildings, of books and blueprints scattered on the floor of offices.

I was in Cologne five or six days ago and found it to be, despite the publicity, proportionately not more ruined than many of the cities I've seen—which is still plenty. Somehow, despite all destruction, the city's skeleton still manages to reveal its greatness and inherent grace. Bomb bursts in the roads have left the trolley tracks sticking crazily in the air. Here, as elsewhere, the poor broken cream-colored trolley cars stand in forlorn rows wherever they happened to be the last time the power broke down (a long time ago), with their windows all smashed, their sides dirt-stained, and the "Occupied" sign still hanging out in front. A couple sits on a park bench at the Kaiser Wilhelm Platz, near the bruised but still imposing Opera building; down at the front, on the river bank a few blocks away, an occasional gun goes "bang." (I didn't get a chance to get up close to the Cathedral, but I got a look at it from several blocks' distance.)

Another expedition some time ago took me to a Dutch town which had recently been liberated [Venlo]. Although great parts of it, notably in the business district, were quite deserted, it had been lavishly decorated with great red, white, blue and orange streamers in honor of a visit by Queen Wilhelmina (just like a Potemkin village, I thought). I had expected to find it more depopulated than it was, and I hadn't counted on the possibility of there being kids.

We walked through a side street in a residential district and were beset by a horde of eager babies requesting chocolate. Luckily I had a bar, which was split into the maximum possible number of pieces. Gee, the looks on the faces of some of those kids! There are no words to describe the expression of a four-year-old boy tasting chocolate for the first time. My friend Eddie [Du Bois] had a pack of chewing gum, and when he distributed it, one little girl actually started to eat her morsel, which shows how newly liberated they really were. [I mention all this mainly in order to say that it was a good feeling to be back for a little while in a country where one could smile at people and talk to kids and feel that one was among completely human beings again.]

German propaganda on a public bulletin board: an appeal for volunteers for the Dutch Waffen-SS, showing a group of jolly laughing soldiers; a long list of Albion's perfidies to Holland, including the rape of New Amsterdam and the Boer War, thus proving that Holland's place in the present conflict is with Germany against her traditional enemy, England; a poster titled "They call it liberation," showing a hand emerging from a sleeve marked with the stars and stripes—clutching the throat of an unidentified Nordic whose tongue extends helplessly; a picture of a row of air raid casualties lying outside a bombed building with the caption, *"Ze hebben gebombardeert"* ("They have bombarded—") then with the list starting "Rotterdam, Amsterdam, 'Gravenhaagen. . . ." That is fine irony; I don't think the Dutch will forget so easily the German destruction of Rotterdam after their surrender.)

One of our boys came up with a story that points up one of the innumerable small ethical conflicts and contradictions involved in the larger problem of Germany. I have mentioned to you the existence of a Displaced Persons Center in which former slave laborers are awaiting shipment and eventual repatriation. Some of these Russians, perhaps stimulated by the homemade potato vodka which they manufacture and consume in large and poisonous quantities, accosted a German girl, took away her bicycle, and lacerated her legs in the process.

Suppose one of us had been there. Almost without exception, not as a soldier, but as someone brought up in the spirit of legality and of fair play among individuals, he would have intervened. Yet I think he would have a hard job explaining to those Russians that a monstrously huge crime on an impersonal social scale does not warrant retribution on the lower level of individual relations.

The boys who went to a historic Passover *seder* brought back a number of boxes of matzos, which I now devour with my midnight cup of hot noodle-soup. This will prove that I am again domesticated. I have covered with cardboard the broken panes of my window, which fronts the village street, from which passing civilians level curious stares.

I have been continuing with a certain amount of reading, although I have much less time for this than formerly. I'm now engaged on the early short stories of Thomas Mann, who is delightfully sentimental without being maudlin, and who reminds me very much of the young Joyce of "Dubliners." I waded through about 150 pages of Alfred Rosenberg's "Myth of the Twentieth Century," supposedly the second most important exposition of Nazi ideology after "Mein Kampf."[6] The stuff reads like the pseudo-scientific horror articles in Hearst's *American Weekly* ("Predicts De-Atomization of Earth in Thirty Years" etc.) with the author proving that the Nordic Germans (who from time to time adopted such pseudonyms as "Persians," "Greeks," "Romans," etc.), are actually descended from the inhabitants of Atlantis. Just think that for twelve years a nation of 80 million lapped up this nonsense!

"Elsewhere in Germany," April 7, 1945: On the roads one passes truckload after truckload of German prisoners moving back from the front. They're packed together like sardines and don't look very happy. The roads are also full of liberated prisoners and slave laborers of every European nationality, marching along, living off the countryside, heading in the general direction of home. Many of the Russians and Poles are simply hanging around waiting for the war to end so that they can go home directly instead of by the long way around through Belgium and France.

Roermond, like Venlo [both in the Netherlands], was a front line town for four months but is still comparatively intact. Before they left each of these towns the Germans blew up the main church, just for spite. Nice people!

Bielefeld, April 18, 1945: We live quite comfortably, as usual, this time in a mountain lodge [The Hünenburg in the Teutoberg forest]. I share a room with four other boys and from our window we have a marvelous view of the surrounding countryside. There is no escaping the fact that Germany is a beautiful land and a rich land. If only the people were different! I never cease to be amazed at the contrasts one constantly finds between places that have been bombed or

In newly liberated Venlo, 1945, the author *(left)* with Edward Du Bois.

shelled into shambles and others, not very far away, that are new and fresh and well cared for, and never seem to have been involved in the war at all. Somehow I just can't feel happy when I see once-splendid cities like Münster or Hanover reduced to ugly heaps of rubble. Perhaps among the worst things the Nazis did was to bring about the destruction of Germany.

Moral Dilemmas

April 23, 1945: Here I am, installed in a castle once more, with a feudal Prussian village clustered around its walls. [This was the estate of Count von Gneisemann, east of Magdeburg.]

April, 1945: I do not cease to be greatly depressed by the devastation I see, maybe because I am a city boy, a lover of houses and busy streets with many vehicles and hurrying people. Here are cities with the hearts knocked out of them, cities that were old and great and populous and beautiful, now heaps of brick and junk, streets that are shoveled paths cleared through the wreckage, world-renowned parks and squares with the grass running wild and the statues melted down for cannon, with the lawns marred by bomb craters and trenches, cities where the people spend half their daytime waiting on queues before the few boarded-up food shops. It knocks the breath out of me to see this, again and

The author striking a pose at a German tank trap on the Siegfried Line.

again. How strange it is to ride at night through the streets of a great ghost city, with the moonlight eery on the skeleton walls of buildings and no man's tread on the pavements. It frightens me to see the endless factory chimneys cold and idle, the plants ravaged and dead, to see all this endless productive capacity lying still, mangled and useless for the building of joy and plenty for all mankind.

I am beginning to question my moral right to ignore Germans, to refuse a child the smile which my heart would give him, to avoid returning the nod and salute of a citizen on the street. The old man sees us coming across the courtyard. He runs halfway back across it and opens the door for us with a bow. Must I deny him a *"Danke"* even though his entire action is deeply offensive to me: the obsequity is the obverse side of the master-slave relationship which he in a collective sense has enforced on others; he renders to me what he would expect if he were conqueror.

The middle-aged woman enters the G.I.-occupied house and when I attend to her business in German, begins to inquire about her son, who is a POW in New York. She cries, and I must comfort her and tell her that her son is well off and that he will come home soon after the war ends and that he won't be sent to Siberia to work for the Russians, as she fears. Yet coldly, objectively, I realize that there would be nothing more salutary for the peace of the world and for the denazification of Germany than to have the woman's boy, whom she dearly loves, and millions of other dearly loved and loving people, away from home for several years, perhaps working for the Russians and Poles and French.

In my present abode I am acutely conscious of the really fundamental way in which any assault on Fascism's hold over Germany must be attacked. I live again in a castle, vastly more lavish and pretentious than the one in which I spent my Belgian winter, a castle which might serve as the prototype for the Prussian Junker estate. From the walls of its great rooms and hallways the huge portraits of gorgeously uniformed ancestors of the present Count scowl at us. The rugs on the floor are thick and red, the furniture ornate, solid and covered with plush in a variety of hideous tints. Everywhere are vases, old prints with titles in Latin, French and English, bric-a-brac from a dozen periods of style, handworked ashtrays, lamps with grotesquely great shades, thick curtains of imposing size and texture. Before the castle the lawn stretches green and lush, with gay flower beds set in it; the avenue from the main gate is lined by ancient and stately trees.

When we "found" this place (I was in the scouting party with our C.O.) a small table indoors was set tastefully for afternoon tea, the Count wore the easy jacket and golfing trousers of the country squire, and a swastika emblem in his hat. He has a large library and a radio-phonograph (removed for the duration of our stay, together with all other valuables); it must have been a pleasant easy life for him before our arrival, with the war very far away indeed. Beyond the subsidiary dwellings, the servants' quarters, the barns and stables and haylofts and sties and pens which ring the castle, beyond the crenellated walls, lie the fields and forests which are the ancestral fiefs, and the village which nestles at the base of the castle hill like an appendage or excrescence. [Since this estate was located in what became the Soviet zone, and later the German Democratic Republic, the Count could not have enjoyed his possessions very much longer.]

In the fields the Polish slaves still labor on the lord's land. (They have been told that they must continue to work if they wish to eat, despite the American occupation,—this by the old Burgomaster, who was in office when we first came). It gave me a strange feeling to ride down a narrow country road and pass a large group of peasant women still clad in their colorful Eastern European costumes. The contrast between their lives and those of the inhabitants of the fine castle with its spires and towers brought to my mind the contrasts I found in the large steel mill in Bielefeld between the sumptuous directors' offices and the miserable quarters of the slaves. There is nothing in any purely political superficial plan for the rehabilitation of Germany that would eliminate the focus of power, resolve the contradictions that have provided the matrix for Fascism's growth. No plan will be at all effective unless it cuts deeply at the present social and economic roots.

One thing of which I become increasingly aware is the fact that one can make generalizations about the Germans only up to a certain point. Not in any age group or social class can one find a unanimity of opinion or corruption or guilt. Each individual by virtue of his own complex of experience retains allegiance to Nazi principles in a variously modified form. It is significant to remember that in Germany, as everywhere, the average person does not give complete allegiance to any value or idea. He may accept it for all outward and pragmatic purposes but unadmitted even to himself are seeds of doubt and disbelief that may at a point of crisis or change of authority grow to sudden maturity and reduce the formerly dominant notions to secondary status. I can therefore readily believe that the extreme civility of most civilians in the great stretches of Germany over which I have travelled is "sincere" to the extent that it is coupled with an inner desire to adapt to new conditions.

I am quite ready to believe that in most of the conquered areas the ordinary person has rejected at least some of the outer symbols of the Third Reich, whether it be the personality of the Führer, or more likely the machinery of the Nazi party. Yet the terrible thing to realize is that this rejection is a completely superficial one. Dr. Goebbels and Co. have done their job very well, and over a period of many long formative years. The whole Nazi ideology, the notion of race, of national biological community, of the inferiority of the Eastern peoples, the complete network of lies and vicious rationalizations which supported the structure of the Fascist state: this all remains deep in the minds of the Germans, not as something which is identified with Nazism, but as something which is identified with truth, something empirically valid like the weight of lead or the color of cloth.

This is demonstrated in innumerable little ways. Posters put up by one firm cite the authority of American military law concerning punishment of looters, and call on the *"deutsche Volksgenossen"* (German racial comrades—a typically Nazi phrase, which is repeated simply because it has passed into the accepted practice of the language) to surrender the goods they have stolen. There are constant expressions of astonishment that the Americans in their dealings with civilians favor the inferior uncouth Poles, Yugoslavs and Russians over the civilized Germans. The problem of identifying all of the Nazi notions with the Nazi symbols, of stabilizing and channelizing the German sense of guilt—that is the main educational task for the future. The force of circumstance itself will serve to topple the symbols; it is up to us to see that the symbols accurately represent the ideas and deeds in the popular mind.

Always I must return to the thought and sight of Europe marching West along the dusty roads of Germany. The antique trucks and Wehrmacht cars flying red or French or Dutch or Polish flags and marked "France Paris" "Frenchman prisoner of war," "Holland there is no place like home" or simply "CCCP" [USSR in the

Cyrillic alphabet] with a hammer and sickle; the men on bicycles, or trudging along on foot, with their worldly goods in knapsacks, marching through rain and cold and unfriendly provinces to freedom and home. Nothing strikes one so sharply with Germany's terrible responsibilities as the knowledge of so many human fates torn up and twisted.

Such a mad strange picture-book land is this country: there are little old houses painted pale blue and pink and cream, with the wall beams outlined in rich deep brown—there are towns with ancient solid block stone churches, with tottering but well-kept burgher houses from the sixteenth century, gabled, with overhanging second stories, with walls and woodwork elaborately festooned with designs and decorations,—color and form and savor of age and life and loveliness to gladden the heart and eye. In Hanover these buildings lie smashed and merged in a general devastation. In this country there is only sadness in the sustained contemplation of pleasure. Perhaps some day soon I shall be able to work out these thoughts to my own satisfaction.

Now the great [military] drives are ended and the war grinds to its close. Again I fear the beginning of a period of ennui and restlessness until the ponderous machinery of the Army begins to roll us forth into new endeavor. I am fairly well satisfied with what my part has been thus far. Our outfit has won the Meritorious Service Plaque, a distinction which I am proud to feel we have earned and which I have done my share in earning.

Military Government

April, 1945: I want to communicate while they are still fresh in my memory and my enthusiasm some of the changes in my perspective that have taken place since yesterday. They grow out of my experiences as an interpreter for an organization establishing military government in this area. (This was voluntary, on my free time.) The area involved covers only a few villages and small towns, but the problems and personalities encountered here are representatives of much wider issues and groups. After all this time of observing no more than the obvious, the outer veneer of Germany, I have come, as I also did in Belgium, to penetrate to the sensitive living core of thought and emotion with which a country reacts to a time of great crisis. All I see and learn increases my awareness of the complexity of the forces at work here, and substantiates my previously arrived-at notions regarding proper solutions to the great problems, solutions that are as evident and logical as they are unlikely to be carried out.

I spent most of the day in the office of the military government unit, the *"Kommandantur,"* the Germans call it. As you have probably read, the procedure in setting up military government is for our authorities to appoint new public officials who bear the burden of administration. Nonetheless the halls of the MG are continually full of scuttling people with a vast variety of errands. They actually represent a cross-section of Germany, because there is no small town in this country that does not contain a great proportion of individuals evacuated from big cities that have been bombed, or occupied sooner by the allied armies.

Here are two girls from one city who were picked up on the road without a pass after they had walked the thirty miles (in one day) to visit the mother of one of them (they are given passes and a warning).

A young priest wants permission to visit his superior in a town outside the normal limits of circulation. He is an extremely insipid, self-consciously holy person, who considers himself to have been a really valiant fighter for human rights because he had sung masses even for Poles. (The Polish slaves were permitted to go to church once a month, with no Germans present). In order to show me how enlightened he is, he proclaimed tremulously, "I believe in the equality of all human souls before God, even of the Poles, even—" he hesitated, "yes, even of the Negroes." "Even of the Jews?" I asked cunningly. He drew himself up as though he were preparing to deliver himself of a weighty and just discovered truth, *"Ja! Auch die Juden!"* [Yes, the Jews too.]

There was a nut—a dark, somewhat pretty, dumpy girl evacuee of 22—who ran into the office, tightly clutching a peanut butter sandwich which she had somehow swiped from the kitchen while waiting to be admitted. She put her sandwich down on the table, sat down, started to cry, reached for her peanut butter sandwich and ate a few bites, started to laugh and suddenly launched into a blue streak of the fastest talking I have ever heard from anyone, in any language. She said that someone had sent her to find out about the cigars that were being distributed to holders of smoking ration cards. I asked her a few questions and she became frightened and came on the verge of tears, then suddenly brightened up and said, "I am so hungry and thirsty and I would like to smoke. Give me some cigarettes." I asked her what work she had been doing since her evacuation (in February). She refused to answer, and when I repeated the question insistently she swooped on her sandwich and ran precipitously out of the room.

Among the visitors was a stocky cruel-faced man of about 60, the richest farmer in the village and a retired officer, Herr T. His house had been taken over for the *Kommandantur*, and he removed most of the furniture, but not the large library of Nazi works and books glorifying militarism. (One number of the official German Army publication, *Die Wehrmacht*, is titled "We fought in Spain" and shows on its cover a stirring picture of German soldiers heading into battle under the Spanish Fascist flag.)

This man, who was *Ortsbauernfuehrer* [farmer leader of the locality: the Nazis gave the largest landowner in each community dictatorial jurisdiction over the others] is being temporarily continued in office (more of this later). He had been personally responsible for the death of a Polish woman who was sent home from the hospital seriously ill (as a Pole she could naturally not remain there) with orders that she remain in bed for several weeks. He had ordered her out to work in the fields, where of course she died immediately. He had her body put in the stable, where it lay for three days without burial.

Herr T. still barks instead of speaking but his bark is somewhat subdued. He was one of a whole slew of petty Nazi party members with whom I had to deal; how cringing, vacuous and contemptible they were now, without their impressive uniforms, their armbands, daggers, pistols and all the other paraphernalia of membership in the Great Horde of the Supermen!

What the foreign slaves had to suffer from these masters is something that cannot be described and unfortunately cannot be revenged in most cases. This suffering was part of a whole vast aching pattern of degradation, for which individuals can always disclaim responsibility. Beatings and hunger were the constant elements in this pattern, as was the treatment of these people as subhumans and the continual pressure on their self-respect. If a German spoke to one of them he had to stand at attention. Several cases came to my attention of Poles or Russians who had been given insufficient or improper medical treatment by the German doctors.

I spoke with, or rather listened at some length to some Polish women whom the Germans had shipped here a few months ago just before the fall of Warsaw to the Russians. They were speaking in Polish, and it was difficult for me to follow exactly what they were saying. They had been in Warsaw during the days of the Ghetto and had seen the Germans hurling children from the roofs of buildings. One of the women had had both parents, her husband and her children killed. They talk hot bloody streams of language, as though they want to spread their hate, instill it in you deeply, and then suddenly they just stop and shake their heads and shudder, "I can't talk of it."

My most voluble informant on all subjects concerning the foreign workers was Mischa, who had been a lieutenant in the Red Army. He is a little man of 28 with a broad pleasant Russian face, who now wears undersized cast-off clothes made of brown imitation leather embellished with a large red star enclosing a white hammer and sickle. He was a war orphan from the last war, was brought up in a state asylum, was sent by the *Komsomol* to the Caucasus at the age of 16 in 1933 to help in the collectivization program. (He compares the conditions of chaos prevailing there at that time with present conditions here). He later became an auto mechanic by trade.

In 1941 his unit was surrounded by the German breakthrough in the Ukraine; it fought its way out through the swamps at night to join another Soviet pocket but he was eventually wounded and captured. Like many other captured Soviet soldiers he was not given the status of a military prisoner but simply made into a civilian slave and put to work on a German farm. The problem on which he came to see us was that all workers, foreign and German, had been asked by MG to return to their jobs temporarily, and it was obvious that the foreign laborers would refuse to go back to certain employers. I was interested to observe Mischa's conduct toward Herr T., who of course was one of these same employers; although the tables were now turned he acted in a completely cold, proper gentlemanly manner.

In the three years during which Mischa had worked in this area he had come to acquire very great familiarity with local personalities and the local situation. I was particularly interested, therefore, to find out whether there were "good" Germans here too. It was thus that I came to find out about the men who have given me new hope and confidence in the eventual redemption of Germany and Europe. There were five of them whom I met, some through Mischa's good offices, some because they were on their way, independently, to protest against existing evils which have since been corrected.

The most striking personality of the five is W., a handsome, sharp-featured man who is probably in his early fifties, though he has been worn and aged by his experiences. Like all the others, he is a skilled workman, who has worked for many years in Berlin or other large cities as well as in his native town. Before 1933 a member of the KPD [German Communist Party], he continued to be active in anti-Nazi circles and was rewarded with two periods of imprisonment, one of four years and one of fifteen months (he was in prison, awaiting trial, when the American armies freed him). He thinks clearly, sharply and forcefully, and his speech expresses this forcefulness and the enormous strength of his inner convictions. I was impressed by the fact that for him, as well as for the others, in varying degrees, his specific acquaintance with local people and problems is combined with a completely worldly outlook. He is a man who might with no difficulties of adjustment appear on a national political stage rather than on that of the local community with which he is now concerned.

What impressed me immediately about these five men was that unlike all the craven little people, temporarily entrusted by MG with posts of civil authority, they met and talked to us Americans like *men*, like equals, who regarded us in the most genuine way as liberators (a feeling I had not yet had in Germany) but who felt—that we as they had a responsibility to the cause of anti-Fascism—a responsibility which they had a right to call to our attention.

Of the other four men, two had been SPD [Social Democratic Party] and two KPD before the advent of Nazism, but during the last twelve years all party differences have lost validity and have broken down completely. There is now, at least in the middle and left, a united anti-Nazi coalition among the rank and file, a coalition that contrasts with the partisan wranglings of the exiled politicians. (Remember the story of the Social Democratic leaders who for years and years have held regular Friday night meetings in New York and argue incessantly about who will be sub-Minister of what in the postwar German government?) A vigorous anti-Nazi German authority can be formed only from the ranks of those who have remained under the Fascist yoke and who have had the courage to retain their intellectual freedom from it and to fight against it. The five men here were not merely perfectly informed regarding the political and military developments through the years (having listened to the allied radio stations) but were in the closest touch with events in their own community and in Germany from the inside.

The type of organization which they had been able to maintain was necessarily of but the loosest kind, being, I gather, more informational than activist. I pointed out to them that there had been some concern in the West over the fact that although flourishing underground movements had existed in all the occupied countries, there was none to speak of in Germany. They answered that the repression in Germany had been utterly incomparable with anything anywhere else. One could trust no one, not even his wife. W.'s mother-in-law, a woman in her seventies, has been imprisoned for eleven years because she at one time was active in the *Rote Hilfe* (the Communist social benefit society). Spies were everywhere. They began to recite the names and horrors of the concentration camps; they knew them all, dozens of which I had never heard of.

I think that the hours I spent with these men were perhaps the first in which they had been able in a free and unguarded atmosphere to talk themselves out all together. And thus it came, the whole terrible story of Germany, the infamy, the deprivation and the degradation, of the work which was slavery and then of the war. D. is also in his fifties, a big man, strong with coarse good-natured features. Twice as he spoke he choked and broke down in his hatred and anguish. He recalled how in March 1933 he had stood in the squares of Berlin wearing a placard reading, "Who votes for Hitler votes for War," and how he had been stoned and spat upon. And then how the war had come, how they had screamed for war, those Nazis in their great mass meetings to which admission was reserved for bearers of Party buttons (the same Party buttons which got you butter when others had lard, which got you a seat in the movies when others had to stand, which got you all the miscellaneous little privileges of life). Yes, the war and the bombings, and the fine beautiful cities lying in ruins and ashes.

But the worst of what the Nazis have done, I said, is what they have made of the German people, their corruption of the German mind. In this they agreed, particularly with regard to the youth (many of whom, they commented, are dead). But they do not feel that the situation is hopeless, even enough it takes years of indoctrination to overcome, and the best proof to me of their feeling is the degree of energy, concern, and enthusiasm with which they approach this problem. I was interested to know their opinion as to the number of people in Germany who share their views, and they assured me that they were by no means the only ones, even in their own towns. As they spoke, and with the background of everything else I have seen, I would divide the population of occupied Germany somewhat as follows:

(a) A small group of people like these, who have managed to maintain their ideological integrity and who are now ready and willing to take an active role in the rehabilitation of Germany;

(b) An appreciably larger segment of the community which has been more or less covertly critical of the Nazis and the war, which now has openly rejected the symbols of Nazism (though it has not maintained sufficient political consciousness to be able to throw over the Nazi ideas which to some degree persist in their minds) and which will form the mass support for the small activist pro-democratic blocs;

(c) Starting from the opposite end, there are all the people who were involved in the Nazi privilege structure: the officials, the people whose business or material welfare was directly associated with their political role. All such Nazi activists, in number probably equal to or somewhat larger than the first-mentioned group, continue to be a positive menace to our military authority and to any democratic German authorities which are set up;

(d) The much larger number of people who have fallen completely for Nazi ideology and will never reject it but whose convictions are not sufficiently intense or well-formulated to make them a positive danger to us;

(e) This leaves the significantly large group of people in the middle, people who have never been politically active, who have accepted quite willingly the Nazi regime and its ideology, who have been the supporters of the Hitler state, but who are still capable of being shown, if the proper pressures are applied, that there are other ways of organizing society.

In the haste of establishing military government in the tens of thousands of German towns and villages the rule of thumb employed appears to have been to appoint as burgomaster someone with "business experience" who is not obviously tainted with an activist Nazi background. This was the case in our village, as has undoubtedly been true in many places and instances. It was in protest against this that W. and the others appeared in our office. They pointed out the importance of effecting a housecleaning at the earliest possible moment and were particularly concerned about the attitude of the undecided middle portion of the population who would be, according to our policy, either cynical or vaguely approving regarding the efforts of the small pro-democratic bloc to attack the vestiges of Fascist power and symbolism. Happily they met an MG officer and interpreters who understood the sense of what they were saying and saw to it that the situation was corrected in a perfectly satisfactory way.

I am greatly concerned, however, about the way in which this problem will be attacked on a much larger scale. My attitude regarding the responsibility of the German people as a whole for the frightful misdeeds wrought by Nazism remains unchanged. I am more clearly conscious than before that there are within the body of the German people a group of politically moral individuals who can be trusted and counted on to work on behalf of democracy, and much larger numbers of individuals who are in one way or another salvageable.

I feel intensely that the success with which Nazism is destroyed is in good part dependent on the degree to which the destruction proceeds from some sort of revolutionary activity on the part of Germans; by that I don't mean militancy or political revolt—Germany is much too totalitarian, too beaten and broken, too subjugated to one authority or another to allow that; I mean simply that Germany is intellectually and emotionally in a ferment; people are forced by events to reconstruct and reevaluate events and ideas that had never before been called into question; we have it in our power as conquerors to guide and channel this ferment and to use it as an instrument of our rule (i.e. in the trial of war criminals).

If we proceed on the basis that a man must be a member of the German equivalent of the Rotary or Kiwanis in order to hold public office we will kill the prestige and potentialities of such small groups here as have consistently opposed Nazism from within. If we proceed to ignore the interrelationship of economic and political controls we may as well resign ourselves to the prospect that Fascist ideas will persist and Germany will continue to be a problem child among the nations for many decades more than she might otherwise be.

Just one example of what I mean, in specific terms; part of my duties consisted of rounding up a truckload of men who had been in the Army and had been furloughed home with wounds. These were to be taken to German military hospitals and eventually to PW camps. Among these men were two who were released by the higher headquarters to which they were first taken, one of them being Johann A., a good-looking blond boy of about 18, who had lost a foot in an accident while taking basic training. Of course when the men had been loaded up in the truck, before the town hall, all their families and friends had been there to see them off with packages and greetings; they were off on a great new journey into unknown fate. Johann, who, I later discovered, was one of the most fanatical members of the *Hitler Jugend* [Youth] in his town, simply could not believe it when I told him that he was being taken back home. He kept stammering to his companion, "Now you see what stories people can tell." Of course his return proved to be quite an event; his girl happened to be in the main street when the truck stopped and she kept saying, "I'm going crazy [with joy]! I'm going crazy!" I mention this incident not for its anecdotal interest but because here was a specific instance in which crisis had provoked at least a reexamination if not yet a change of ideas: The HJ had apparently misrepresented the truth regarding American treatment of war prisoners; might it not also have misrepresented other truths, as the Americans and Herr W. claim? Human beings, I continue to learn, are infinitely complex and interesting.

The Final Days

"Elsewhere again in Germany," April, 1945: Mail has neither come in nor gone out; that is a very small price to pay for the great galloping advances by our armies which are finally bringing an end to the war. Now at last we are in the core, the heart of Germany, and on us falls the weight of a whole new set of experiences, not merely of another country, but of a system of life and of character development that we can understand from the outside only.

Until now it has been fortunately possible for me to do my daily job in the war without any sense of personal impact as an individual soldier on the lives of other individuals. I have been part of a great relentless machine manufacturing death and destruction, yet except in rare instances my part in the drama of war has been anonymous and detached, or else defensive and passive. One comes to take shells and buzz bombs as calamities of nature; there is no human contact involved; one plays no actively destructive role. In Germany this has all changed. We are here as a conquering enemy. Our safety and comfort involve suffering or discomfiture for Germans. Even the rear echelon soldier is continually required to behave by the habits and morals of war rather than by those of the civility to which he is accustomed.

I lounge by the mess hall of another outfit, eating a sandwich (lunch). Two women walk up to see the "Kommandant." He has difficulties, so I interpret. The women are middle-aged, homely, pleasant-looking. They smile nervously and somewhat falsely as they talk. Two soldiers have come into their house and taken the radio away. "So?" I say coldly. The ingratiating smiles grow a little more tense. "We only wanted to know, are they allowed to do it? Could we have a receipt for it?" I translate for the lieutenant, who says, "Tell 'em T.S. [tough shit, Army talk for "too bad!"]" and goes about his business. I tell them we know nothing about their radio and there's nothing to be done about it. The false smiles continue, augmented now by little bows. "Good. Good." "No!" I shout angrily, "It isn't good! War isn't good! You Germans have to learn that!" They say yes, yes and depart unhappily. I know I have done right, and yet something inside me feels upset and uncertain about my right to lecture middle-aged women regarding the facts of political life.

If a military unit in Germany needs billets, it selects its house and dispossesses the inhabitants on as many minutes' or hours' notice as it wishes to give them. When we had to find quarters last for a small group of our men, we picked a likely building and told the woman who answered the door that she would have to be moving. She started to tremble. We relented, being Detachment D, etc., and asked where the old Nazi Burgomaster of the village lived. The inhabitants of the house we had chosen now began to breathe with fresh hope. The Burgomaster had fled and the Americans had occupied his house, but his deputy was still here, and they could show us where he lived.

The deputy's house, comfortable and well-kept like almost all the middle-class German houses I have seen, was duly occupied by us on 24 hours notice, but I was troubled, even though we were dealing with people whom we knew to be Nazis and profiteers from the Nazi power. The wife kept striking her fist into the palm of her hand in anguish, and a bombed-out young refugee woman who had been staying there insisted on taking our officer inside to show him her baby, thinking that this would soften our hard hearts. I know that we needed that house for our boys to stay in, I know that the Germans whom we kicked out will find shelter elsewhere. Yet it is not good to feel that even if only temporarily you have cut human beings off from their roots, from their home, from all the small loved amenities of life. Undoubtedly in the last half year my work has helped to break up many homes, to kill young men and bring agony to their women, but it has always worked through devious abstracted channels. Now I am personally an agent of woe, and this is no source of joy to me.

The two prisoners I took to the stockade yesterday were deserters, wore civilian clothes and reported to give themselves up, with their personal possessions wrapped up in several ungainly bundles. When I came to take them they were sitting comfortably on the steps of the house talking to the boys and smoking American cigarettes. (One of them had lived in America and spoke English.) They were a little brown Austrian of 43 and a big blond dumb-looking peasant from the local region. The little guy kept saying that he wished he had stayed in America, but he couldn't become a citizen because he had jumped ship to get there.

The big guy kept quiet. I found out that he had been in the Wesel pocket [a key point of late German resistance] and that he had fought at the Russian front in '41. "We know what you German soldiers did in Russia," I told him, mentioning a few facts. "Yes," he said, "At Krivoi Rog eighty of our men machine-gunned 4,000 Russian civilians, women and children." "You were there," I said. "I didn't do it," he answered. "I can look any man in the eye and tell him I had no part of it." And he looked me in the eye for many seconds. "You didn't do anything to stop it. You'll all have to pay now for what you've done," I told him, and he said nothing. We rode in silence and I had the gun in my hands, with a bullet in the chamber. We turned them in at the PW enclosure.

Only a few hours before they had been free and individual, each a man with his own problems and his own story. Behind the barbed wire and concrete walls of the stockade they became nameless parts of a great subdued mass of green uniforms, to be incarcerated and frustrated for months or years. On these two lives I have had a direct and negative impact, and the awareness of this startles me a little.

The PW enclosure, incidentally, is a weird and rather terrible sight. The prisoners, packed like sardines in the trucks from the front, arrive in a constant deluge. The men are dusty and battle-damaged, and one sees among them kids who can not possibly be older than 15 or 16. It is almost comical to see how many of the officers, even in captivity, sport shiny boots and well-pressed uniforms. Sitting in the officers' cage was the very model of a German Major-General, with his fancy uniform all scarlet and gold and the inevitable monocle in his eye; he looked like a caricature of what one might imagine a high Prussian officer to be.

Among the numerous prisoners in civilian clothes were several officers, dignified looking "gentlemen" in the German equivalent of Brooks Brothers clothing, carrying homburg hats and bulky briefcases. They looked as though they were going to a directors' meeting. It was good to see the bastards in the stockade, but unfortunate to realize that so many of them were still alive and to reflect that in our prison camps they will continue to parade about as gentlemen of leisure entitled to all the privileges of military courtesy. One thing that sickened me: an SS man, standing out in his black uniform. To think that one of these murderers will become just another PW and be lost in the vast maw of our prison camps, eventually to be released and continue on his way!

The one prisoner I captured (with Ed Du Bois) was also a deserter. He was a high-ranking non-com and spoke excellent English. We discovered him quite by accident, sitting with his wife in a secluded country café that appeared to be functioning just as though the war had never existed. I happened to notice him through the window. When he saw me he turned several shades of white. It was so obviously suspicious that I would have felt like a damn fool if I had just walked by, so I beckoned to him to step outside and called to Ed. I asked him for his identification and he produced his *Rassenschein* ["Ancestry Pass"], a record of "racial purity" that all the Germans carry with them. We asked for his military status and he told us what it was. We asked him whether he realized that under the rules of land warfare he could be shot as a spy, since he was wearing civilian clothes. He blanched and fumbled and said, "All the German boys are doing it now, you know. I thought I would just do like all the boys. I've worn the damned uniform long enough."

Ed and I held a conference about what to do, and there wasn't any choice but to turn the guy in. His wife turned out to be in her seventh month of pregnancy and he kept asking us to let him spend the night with her, but we had committed ourselves already so we told him to go inside and say goodbye and make his preparations (all this as politely as the circumstances permitted). He came out at last and said to Ed (I was watching the other side of the house) with complete deathly fearful seriousness, "I am at your disposal. Are you going to shoot me?" Ed was so shocked he could only blurt out, "My God, man, I'm not a German!" We brought the prisoner to the enclosure and came back to the café to assure his wife that he was all right and that that it was a good thing that he was taken now rather than later. An unmitigated mess.

It is uncanny to see how the Wehrmacht and the whole rotten Nazi structure continue to operate right behind our lines. The German military hospitals we have overrun continue to operate as always, in many cases without guard. The patients are treated by their own doctors and medics, who continue to function just as they did before our arrival. We actually stopped one arrogant young Nazi in civilian clothes (he presented a 1939 driver's license by way of identification) who said that he was getting his discharge from the Wehrmacht on the following day.

We entered the grounds of one of these German military hospitals, attempting to get medical treatment for a Frenchman, a former prisoner, who had broken his ankle in escaping. The place was full of clean, splendid-looking German soldiers and officers in their green uniforms heavily laden with iron crosses and miscellaneous decorations. One oily-smiling individual, an Oberleutnant, probably a doctor, came forward to greet our lieutenant with a military salute. "Yes sir, is there anything we can do for you, sir?" (Beautiful Oxonian English). The lieutenant explained about the Frenchman, whom we had found with his two buddies driving a Wehrmacht two-cylinder sedan down the road. "Oh, I am so sorry," said the Nazi doctor, "We are only supposed to treat Germans here. You will have to take the man somewhere else. If you had a German I would be very happy to help you out." So we departed on a two-hour search for an American hospital. Our lieutenant returned the Oberleutnant's salute with a sloppy wave and I snarled an obscenity by way of farewell. It is difficult for me to direct my hate of Fascism at personal objects; with ordinary common working people it is almost impossible. The only individuals for whom I can feel a real personal hate are the intellectuals who sold out to Hitler—the doctors and lawyers and teachers and engineers who had the educational background to be able to see through Fascism and who succumbed to it or cooperated with it rather than give up status and position or in order to acquire them.

I rode with the Frenchmen for a long time after we dropped off their injured comrade. Both of them came from small towns in the Vosges and wanted to get back to France *"le plus vite possible* [as quickly as possible]." They had been imprisoned at one of the so-called *Kommandos* in a rural area. Thirty or forty prisoners were apportioned to the farmers of two villages. They worked from 6 o'clock in the morning until 8 or 9 at night, with ten or fifteen minutes off for lunch. At night they returned to their *Kommando*. Despite this they had kept in touch with world affairs, managing occasionally to hear the BBC French broadcasts. The Germans, they said, had made much in their propaganda among the French of the Allied deal with [Vichy's North African satrap, Admiral Jean François] Darlan, and of the rift between the Western allies and the Soviet Union. They observed that the Germans fanatically believed in victory up till about two days before the arrival of American tanks, but noted that there were also some anti-Nazi Germans, "Communists," who rounded up the Nazi leaders and turned them over to the Americans when we arrived.

The German farmer who was the boss of one of the men had aided them to escape when the prisoners were rounded up for a trek to the East during the last few days. He hid them in his barn, brought them food, and even made a little French tricolor for them, which adorned their "liberated" vehicle. One of the Frenchmen told with great earnestness a story told him by a Ukrainian woman who had worked with him on his farm. When the Germans took her town, they took all the Jewish girls and young women, slept with them and murdered them the following morning. There it is, you see. You can't get away from it, this horrible manic ghoul who lurks behind the innocent mask that is the face of every German.

I have never been so sharply aware of the degree to which German Fascism has been an extreme expression of the "free private enterprise" profit system, never so well-prepared to give the lie to those who attempt to equate it with socialist forms of state control. To understand this one must go through a large factory. In the sumptuous directors' offices, beautifully, lavishly equipped with modern furniture, rugs, inspiring blown-up photographs on the walls, one finds the splendid, expensively printed brochure, "Blood and Soil," the photographs of Herr Dr. Bobert, the Hauptdirektor together with the Führer (both smiling graciously), with Grossadmiral Raeder, with Reichsminister Dr. Rosenberg, with Reichsminister Goering. On the shelves are the books where the profits were marked up. The Herr Direktor had an intellectual bias, perhaps.

There is also a small library, including standard reference works in English. Yes, one must see this, and then go through the factory where the latrines are labeled "For Germans Only!" to the barracks where the foreign slaves lived, crowded together in double or triple-decker beds, in filth and desolation, surrounded by barbed wire. Oh, it would make old Henry Ford's heart leap with joy. Super-efficient industrialism!

A truck passed me today pulling a great big trailer, both of them full of just-liberated Russian slaves, one of them waving a big red flag. They were yelling and whooping for joy, happier than any bunch of people I had ever seen in my life. But I think Herr Dr. Bobert would be very sorry to see them leaving him. Actually, when one talks to the Germans, one might think to hear them that we were at war, not with them, but with the Russians and French and all such low uncouth subhuman racial species. They look to us to protect their "property" from the depredations of vandals now released from slavery, they really do. To some degree the rapid advance of our armies must be due to the German fear that if we don't take over the Russians will, and the Russians, unlike us, have a pretty clearcut notion of what the Nazis have coming to them.

As long as I have been in Germany, I have had no contact with any hostile act of resistance. Anyone with whom one has any occasion to speak of course piously disclaims any connection with the Nazis, and sometimes even speaks a few well-chosen words of opposition to them, some of which are undoubtedly genuine. This, to be sure, is deep inside Germany, so deep that it has hardly suffered from the war, in contrast to the places I have been in previously. One might therefore expect bitterness against the Americans to be correspondingly less acute. Naturally they tend to judge us by their own standards. When our jeep runs down the main streets of recently conquered villages, people scurry in all directions to get out of the way and little children race into the safety of their backyards, beyond the range of the Evil Eye.

It is a rather luxurious feeling to be sleeping on a mattress, to have running water, commercial power and a toilet that flushes. We sit in an inn on a height in a marvelous fir forest. The air and the scenery are wonderfully invigorating, the sort of thing that tourists spend lots of money to enjoy. Sure, there's still some of the old tourist Germany left, little towns with cobbled streets and old buildings and lazy canals, towns that the war raced through without a single huff or puff of damage. And there are other old towns, also famed for their picturesqueness and antiquity, towns like Dulmen and Muenster and Wesel, that are heaps of rubble through which the bulldozers have had to plow from end to end to clear the lanes for G.I. traffic.

Our previous abode had been a Nazi headquarters, and the ground beneath it was honeycombed with deep air raid shelters, the famous *"Parteibunker"* where the party big shots whiled away the air-raid hours while the rest of the population sweated it out in less effectively isolated caverns. Our brave warriors liberated a warehouse full of gin several nights ago, and for one evening carousal continued without adulteration, except by small quantities of orange juice. I missed most of it, since I was working, but vast numbers of ordinarily phlegmatic individuals began publicly to declaim the stories of their lives, others began to stage impromptu exhibitions of the noble art of self-offense (with the intervening party invariably becoming involved with one of the participants, the other one in turn intervening pacifically), one of the elite of the administration attempting to fry a pork chop on the floor of his room at 3 A.M. and another one arriving for work the following morning, only to find the walls and ceiling of his office revolving around him like a Steeplechase man-trap. All in all, a wild debauch in the Roman manner. I think the end of the war will be celebrated in a relatively sober fashion.

Several stories of another day I spent with the MG (military government team):
First of all, our anti-Nazi mayor told us the story of Dr. Bohne, the mastermind of the local Nazi machine, and director of the wax factory—an IG Farben subsidiary which is the town's largest industry. Dr. B. is a prosperous-looking

gentleman (the richest man in the area) who speaks good English and reports that he has many friends in England and the U.S. with whom he is anxious to reestablish business connections. He complains to the Americans about our choice for mayor, whom he dismisses as a "Communist." (Actually, in 1937, when the present mayor was released from the concentration camp, B., through the Nazi Labor Office, forced him to work in the wax factory, where his activities could be most effectively supervised.)

B. was already known as a Nazi when he arrived in the town after the [First World] war. (He had served as an officer and then gone back to complete his university course). He proceeded to organize the party during the early years, and played a significant role as liaison agent among the NSDAP [Nationalist Socialist German Workers (Nazi) Party] groups in nearby cities. B. during this time remained constantly in the background, selecting minions like his chauffeur to occupy the official posts, do the dirty work, and take any blame attached. (The chauffeur actually flourished in his job to such a degree that he finally went into business for himself, acquired rich contracts by means of his party connections, and became wealthy).

The wax factory became the nucleus of all Nazi activity throughout the area. Work was obtained only by holders of party membership cards (and jobs were scarce in Germany during the early Depression years) and the employees were sent out on organizing missions on company time. Military drill and practice with firearms were held in the firm's yard. Dr. B. meanwhile continued to play ball with the German big business party, the People's Democratic Party, supporting it financially as well as the Nazis. After the advent of Hitler to power he sought vainly to obtain a good position in Berlin in the Economics Ministry and finally settled back to continue his very free and very private enterprise with a couple of honorary National Socialist titles added to his name.

All this is a very simple little story, but it is beautifully typical of the identification between business and political games that is behind the whole sordid saga of Fascism. The disgusting thing is that Dr. B. has committed no "crime" from the perspective of any "Western" view. He has not killed or tortured anyone, though he has been responsible for the organization of far more murder and torture than any small-fry storm trooper. So now he sits as always in his office in the wax factory, fulminates against the Communists in office, and prepares to establish business connections with his very good friends in Britain and U.S.

We went to see an archenemy of Dr. B.'s, a corpulent hippo-faced landowner who had been a Nazi (he greeted us with the automatic Hitler salute, which he explained away as a local greeting, meaning *"Heil Mahlzeit!"*),[7] although his father-in-law has been murdered in 1934 through Bohne's influence. In true style, this chap protested about the evils of the last twelve years, referred to his great intimacy with a certain non-Aryan Dr. Hirschberg, now in America (Did I happen to know him?), but refused to mention the names of any specific Nazis other than B. on the grounds that B. would get him, or that they were all dead.

In a small village, some twenty miles away, another one of our German anti-Fascists told us, a group of SS came through one evening about a month ago, escorting 300 political prisoners of all nationalities who were being evacuated from the area in the path of the advancing Americans. The prisoners were billeted for the night in a large barn. The following morning about sixty of them managed to bury and hide themselves in the hay. Their absence was noted by the SS, but there was no time for a roll-call, so the rest of the prisoners were marched off. The local authorities were informed and threw a ring around the barn. There were thirty members of the *Arbeitsfront* [the Nazi Labor Front], two policemen and ten members of the *Volkssturm*. These men proceeded to go methodically through the barn and as fast as a prisoner was found he was put to death by shooting or clubbing. The killing continued throughout the day, and in the evening the dead were buried in the village churchyard in a mass grave. The barn was guarded all night, but since there was no sign of life the guard was removed the next morning.

On the following day, the first American troops entered the village and three survivors, a Pole and two Russians, appeared. The *Arbeitsfront* people remained with the retreating German army, from which they will vanish briefly into the charming anonymity of PW camps. The policemen, I suppose, now carry MG [Military Government] armbands, and the *Volkssturm* men have their civilian clothes on and are going about their daily business like the peaceful law-abiding citizens they seem to be, to the naked eye. What's one more atrocity case? People shrug their shoulders.

To impede our advance, the Germans had blown up the bridges over which Hitler's marvelous network of Autobahnen wound through the Alps. Military traffic snaked slowly through the secondary roads, fording streams or crossing them warily over pontoon bridges. Moving in the opposite direction came dispirited refugees. At one point, a fierce-looking red-mustached tank sergeant stood waving his arms at an extended family of aged and very young, in a cart drawn by an ox. "*Raus!*" [*Heraus*, get out] he bellowed, "*Raus!*" In terror, they abandoned the road.

April, 1945: At this point the door opened and various friends and relations burst joyously into the van, remaining for approximately 2½ hours for discussions on many subjects, all of them concerning the effect of the war on our personal lives. From each of us, we reflect, it will have taken five or six of our best years. There will be no "readjustment," one of the fellows says, since readjustment implies a return to past conditions. We must all break new ground, and all of us will be older and altered and with no skills sharp and usable except the skills of Army. Our discussions now invariably involve either our acts and feelings as individuals or else the very highest abstractions of our acts and feelings on a moral and ethical plane. We are completely apolitical, except in the very local sphere. Our news, for weeks, has consisted simply of the bare military facts announced on the radio. We are unable to follow the complex network of paths that the political war takes, either on the world or American scale. Among left [wing] intellectuals at home this must be a time of great bitterness and disillusionment, but I feel that almost instinctively, as something that is the inevitable accompaniment to the conclusion of war, rather than as anything based on specific happenings of which I have knowledge. Since my correspondence has just about stopped since February I have not even had any friendly bird's-eye view of developments on the ideological front.

Yet I am in the midst of a most critical conflict of ideas and attitudes, reflected by confusion in my own mind. As I continue to discover darkest Germany I am seized by strong contradictory impulses. On the one hand I am enormously fascinated by the vast welter of social challenges offered by this great battered disorganized country that our armies have conquered. On the other hand I am filled by a tremendous weariness and revulsion when I contemplate the hopelessly ruined cities and the warped minds.

Chapter 10

A Postwar Assignment

After the Luftwaffe's operations ceased, Flap Dog was given one last assignment: to monitor the Soviets. We had a few Russian speakers, but their skills were minimal, and it is unlikely that they turned up anything of value. This distrust of our close Allies, which seemed senseless to me at the time, indicates in retrospect that someone at the Pentagon was more astute than we realized.

Our armies halted to let the Russians take Berlin, and Hitler committed suicide. From Germany's eastern heartland I was pulled back to the handsome spa city of Wiesbaden in the Rhineland. Along with several others, I was now placed on detached duty with an intelligence unit whose assignment was to capture (before the Soviets could) all the German personnel and documents that might have continuing military interest for us as attention turned to the Pacific Theater of War.

My marching orders, embossed with an impressive seal, are worth reproducing in full, with all the mysterious abbreviations, to illustrate the workings of the military bureaucracy. In true military fashion, they were dated after the fact:

Restricted
HEADQUARTERS
NINTH AIR FORCE ADVANCED
APO 696, U.S. Army
12 May 1945
SUBJECT: Orders

TO: Sgt Leo Bogart, 12088872, Det D, 3rd Radio Sq Mobile (G), attached to PW & X Det, Hq, Ninth Air Force Advanced.

You are placed on temporary duty and will proceed from Hq to PW & X Det, Hq, First Tactical Air Force, (Prov), for the purpose of performing PW & X duties. TDN by MT, mil acft or rail. 60-114 P432-02 A 212/50425.

Travel dir is pursuant to the auth contained in Ltr, Hq, European TO USA, 22 Nov 1944, file 300.4 MPM.

By command of Lieutenant General VANDENBERG:

HARRY E KOCH
Major A G D
Asst Adj Gen
DISTRIBUTION:
2 cys EM concerned
1 cy Det D, 3rd Radio Sq Mobile (G)
1 cy Ninth AF (Attn: AG Pers)
1 cy AG Files

Wiesbaden, May 6, 1945: I am now still in Germany, but a considerable distance behind the front (or what would be considered the front if the war were not in its last throes of expiration). I am on detached service with the Military Intelligence section of the Twelfth Army Group, but I have no idea at all of what my status actually is or of what it is likely to be in the future, immediate and otherwise. Life with this big headquarters is greatly different from what it has been with my little Detachment D; there is much to look back on with a certain amount of nostalgia. With the war's end, old tasks have lost their validity and new ones arise to be done. Paradoxically, our creature comforts were more lavishly attended to in the field than they can be in garrison. That is very reasonable, since our small unit could always take its pick of the best quarters in an area, whereas HQ personnel are simply assigned quarters in whatever section of a city is selected by the brass for its military use. It is disconcerting to be stationed right in a town, with its manifold aspects of life swirling and pullulating all about one temptingly, and to be unable, both from inner and outer compulsions, to participate in it. Hitherto in Germany my existence managed to proceed quite roundly within the limits of our secluded unit; now an altogether new adjustment becomes necessary.

This city has been bombed, but not too heavily, compared with the average German town of its size, and it has been under our occupation long enough for its population to have settled down to a normal, or at least recuperative pattern. On Sunday afternoon it strolls as usual in the parks; it casts only casual glances at the G.I.s who hurry through its business section clanging mess-kits at the noon hour. (In the midst of the chaos it was unsettling to hear someone in an apartment house practicing Bach's "Well Tempered Clavichord.")

In the evening, after curfew, the whores retire to their doorways and windows and take up their posts, ready for business as usual. The kids have learned to say "chewing gum." Damaged stores are repairing their banged up facades. In fifteen years the rubble will have been repaired or torn down altogether,[1] the soldiers will be back from the PW camps and rearing new families, and the inhabitants will be ready to think seriously again about the possibilities for another war.

I have by now seen a great deal of this country, perhaps more than the average

American soldier has had a chance to see. I have devoured so many satisfying landscapes and the sight of so many devastated towns that new beauties and new ruins alike no longer stir me as they ought to do.

Hitler's successor, Grossadmiral Doenitz, surrendered on May 7. The war was officially over.

Displaced Persons

May 7, 1945: Harry's [Yoselowitz] parents have heard from him through the Red Cross.[2] He's a prisoner of war in Germany, but as the war goes now I don't imagine he'll be one much longer. It would be hard to think of anyone more difficult to associate with high adventure. It's difficult to imagine him going back to his desk as a clerk in the municipal court, spending his evenings as of old, listening to swing records or strolling down to the corner to have a beer with the boys. Yet it must be so for him and millions of others, even including those like me on whom the war has had a less violent personal impact.

I can well understand why for so many veterans of the first world war everything that happened afterwards came as a footnote and an afterthought. It is hard for men who have weighed the precious essence of life in their hands to readjust to an existence of unregulated monotony (and to an appreciable degree, of lower living standards. The flying colonel who is offered his old job as office boy, the Negro sergeant who has lived in a German castle and returns to the squalor of a cropper's shack— these are by now classic examples, but they are, nonetheless, to the point).

Harry's imprisonment, at any rate, will not have been unduly long. It bears little in common with the four- and five-year ordeal of the thousands of war prisoners who have now been released by our advancing armies. The roads of Germany now present a truly fantastic sight. First of all, there is our military traffic, the endless convoys moving up, and other convoys coming back, uncovered G.I. trucks packed tight with German PWs. They look gray and haggard and unshaven, and there is nothing for them to look or feel happy about, despite the joyous tone of our propaganda leaflets. The men seem to be middle-aged for the most part; they are in green Wehrmacht or blue-grey Luftwaffe uniforms, with some *Volkssturmmänner* [men] in civilian clothes, and even an occasional woman packed right in with the rest. One looks in vain, either among these Germans, or among the remaining male representatives of the civilian populace, for any examples of the classic Aryan superman prototype. Even for the Germans, that myth must be pretty well out of fashion by now.

Also on the roads one sees German civilians, mostly pushing carts or wheelbarrows, returning to the homes they left while the battle was on. A good part of the time I suppose they find not much more than a heap of bricks and junk to scramble in, for though the war these days moves fast, it also moves furiously, and a town can be leveled in a few days.

But the most impressive sight is that of liberated Europeans on the march home. Afoot or on bicycle, with their belongings in knapsacks, bags, suitcases carried or piled on carts, are the nationals of every country that Germany invaded or conquered since the war began. Some are former slaves, in ragged civilian clothes. Others wear the faded, worn-out uniforms of Russia, France, Belgium, Holland, Yugoslavia, Greece, Poland and Italy. Now at last they are headed West and home, and this homecoming has the dramatic quality of a biblical wandering. Oh, they have waited long for us, they say, and one knows and believes this, because a young man's years go quickly, and these years of war and confinement were lost from the lives of Europe's finest manhood. I feel like someone who sees the two sides of a play whose separate strands meet only at the end. In the towns of France and Belgium I have seen the women patiently waiting, waiting for their men, and now to see these men, brown and worn and gaunt and weary, trudging west on the dusty highways, laughing and pulling their collective baggage wagons!

Each of these individuals has his own story, but all are merged in a great collective story of Europe in exile, transient, disorganized by Fascism. The little Serb who insisted on pumping water for me at the well (he wouldn't release the handle, and he smiled as only a very simple and good person could; he spoke Serbian, while I attempted my tentative Russian) summed it up when he said, "In the Army they made me work hard, but they fed me. The Germans made me slave for them, but they wouldn't give me anything to eat." A Dutchman who had walked all the way from Berlin (no mean distance; he said Berlin was merely rubble, with the population living in the air raid shelters). A group of Frenchmen who hadn't heard from home in two years; you should have seen their expression when I told them that the French army was fighting on German soil. "How is it in France?" they wanted to know, "Do the trains run?" So I told them how it was, that the trains ran, but that it was hard, and that the Boche had left much destruction behind him. Homecoming will be bitter for many of these men, for they will find nothing to which to return.

This may hold true more frequently for the Russians, who have seen among the Germans a standard of living much higher than their own, and who come from those areas of Western Russia and the Ukraine that were most devastated by the Germans. Many of the Russians are simply bumming along for the time being, thinking their chances of returning home are better if they remain where they are until the war ends and they can proceed directly east instead of going to Belgium or France now. They live in deserted buildings or barracks, and roam the countryside "appropriating" food from the German farmers. A couple of our boys stopped a gang of Germans from lynching two Russians who had "found" a chicken. I stopped two men on bicycles riding up the road to our site. "Russki!" one of them shouted. "Where are you going?" I asked in Russian. He answered in half German, half Russian, shaking a brawny bare arm and fist: "From the farmer—bread!"

After a while one simply stops bedeviling oneself about the moral issues involved in such acts. A man is hungry and has no way of eating except by stealing. That perhaps is fundamentally moral. One ought, maybe, to object to the procedure rather than to the end. One ends up with a feeling of callous detachment. There is nothing one is in any position to do except by the insignificant way of personal charity. Thus far in the war the American soldier has not had a conflict in his attitudes. He was fighting in friendly country; his actions toward the enemy were fixed by formula; his posture toward civilians was not supposed to be significantly different from that toward civilians at home.

But now that the army stands deep in Germany, the term "enemy" is extended to civilians, and hostility must underlie all the casual little contacts in which all previous conditions prompt one to be considerate and polite. The easiest way, unquestionably, is to forget the larger issues and to treat individual Germans as ordinary humans. In the long run that doesn't work. I was by no means unperturbed when I had to detour an old blind man, his daughter and her three or four young children (their eyes staring with curiosity and fear) from their customary shortcut home (which went near our [restricted] area), but I don't doubt for a minute that I did the right thing.

I see more and more of Germany and ever more destruction. The Nazi slogans on the walls read, "Our hate, Anglo-Amerika!" and "Death to the invader!" and "Every village, every town a fortress!" and "Hard times, hard hearts!" The newspapers (published up to within a few days of the American occupation) report that in Cologne the American troops have requisitioned food from the civilian population, since their supply system is all screwed up. (I wonder what the writer of that article would give for my last night's supper of steak and French fried potatoes.) It is also announced that the U.S. Army has created special units of Negroes and Jews to be let loose on the defenseless civilian population. The German press also had kind words for Dewey's brave stand against the war-mongering tyrant Roosevelt.

May 9, 1945: So now it is really once and for all officially over. There was no particular celebration here over the announcement of VE-Day. Germany had been dying slowly throughout the past weeks, so the final collapse didn't come as a great surprise.

The order has come out permitting us to take off our leggings and helmets, and I suppose that ties and blouses will soon be standard uniform. Last night Radio Luxembourg played the Beethoven "Missa Solemnis" by way of celebration and Radio Zürich, with delightful Swiss neutrality, the chorale movement of the Ninth Symphony—"All men will be brothers"—tender sentiment. Immediately afterwards I tuned in on Radio Prague, broadcasting in English, "This afternoon the people of Prague [the announcer pronounced it to rhyme with "vague"] were listening to Prime Minister Churchill announce the end of the war, while at the same time German planes were dive-bombing our city. At this moment the Nazi beasts are shelling our hospitals. Please send help! Allied friends, please help Prague!"

That was last night, but now the Prague radio is broadcasting an opera, while Paris gives forth with a tumultuous Mozart piano concerto. Our windows stand wide open and the light shines forth. How wonderful! All over Europe the windows open again and their bright warmth making the night cheerful and friendly! I remember my first English blackout evening at Chorley last summer, with the unrelieved silhouettes of the chimney pots standing out against the gloomy sky, and my horror at Paris's sloppy blackout a couple of weeks after its liberation, and our great concern, during the days of the "Bulge," with the slivers of light that persistently showed at the window edges of our vans. (A match can be seen a mile, and Jerry [the German Air Force] paid us a visit every night.) We saw in every careless peasant's barnyard lamp a secret beacon for the enemy and stopped our jeep to shout warnings, *"Il faut maintenir le camouflage!"* ["Stay camouflaged!"]

So that's over now, and I'm glad even for the Germans. A couple of weeks ago, when hostilities were still very much in progress, I stood on a street corner in Helmstedt while wave after wave of American bombers passed high overhead. Everyone was out on the street looking up and shielding his eyes (it was a bright sunny day), and there was still a bit of nervous tension in the atmosphere. How they must have stood like that, on so many days, with their hearts full of awe and fear! A horde of kids, gathered around us, put on a little show for our benefit, yelling excitedly and pointing at each new formation and some that were entirely imaginary. Unlike the adults, they showed no signs of fright or anger, but reacted in the simple mechanical terms of delight that one might expect of kids anywhere. Now the same bombers, used as transports, I suppose, fly low over the German countryside, and there is no female announcer to proclaim in a sexy, throaty voice, as always, over the "Great-German Radio Network with all of its Transmitters," that "Over the territory of the Reich there is no single enemy air formation." (How often we heard that on the German radio when the planes were actually roaring overhead!)

I don't think we'll have trouble handling the Germans, simply because they have indoctrinated themselves with the notion of order and subjection to authority to a point where it stands as a principle in itself—beyond the Nazi doctrine—and where it can as readily be applied to General Eisenhower and the rest of us as to Hitler and the NSDAP. The spontaneous reactions of the kids are good indications of the attitudes that prevail toward us at home. In Prussia and the Ruhr they were curious, sometimes fearful (the very little ones: "If you don't make wee-wee the American soldiers will come and cut off your legs!") and generally undemonstrative in their reactions. In Southern Germany they stand along the highway, give the V-sign, and ask you for "Schockli" if you stop. Only occasionally can one see a child make a face or a threatening gesture or an unfriendly remark.

But wherever one goes—North, East, South or West—there is destruction and more destruction. Only a very few towns I have seen have escaped it, and those are places of cultural interest without much military or industrial importance—Heidelberg, Helmstedt, Weimar, Lemgo. One enters these places with a bit of a shock. "Why, this is too big a town to be intact! Where are all the ruins?" Heidelberg, for instance, lovely and antique, with the plate-glass windows in its department stores still unbroken! The streets crowded with civilian traffic, the shops (pretty empty but) all open, G.I.s dunking doughnuts in Red Cross coffee in an "exclusive" café while a violin-accordion duet plays Viennese waltzes. [The stacks of the university library ransacked by the same G.I.s; books strewn about, for the pure pleasure of doing mischief. A Puerto Rican unit billeted in Heidelberg castle.]

Heidelberg, May 17, 1945: We have a large house with a sunny veranda. I sleep in a bed with springs, mattress, a pillow and a bedspread (unheard of luxury), eat in a restaurant with real plates and silverware. I have discovered that I am a Staff Sergeant, which means 115 dollars a month.

May, 1945: I am afraid that the group of Germans who will provide the largest most closely knit Fascist bloc in this country after the war will not be the youth but the German PWs now in the U.S. camps. They will be the only group who will not have undergone the revolutionary catharsis of the war's final moments, and they will return with their morale high and their ideology untouched.

In the railroad yards I have seen the cattle-cars marked with the six-pointed Jewish star. But it will be easy for many to forget.

The world seems like a series of lantern slides: forests turning green, curving fields and lush lawns and comfortable brick farmhouses, fruit trees flowering in pink and white. Each scene becomes a static reality. Now Germany is a fairy landscape from a childhood storybook, from the score of Beethoven's "Pastorale Symphony"; now it is the evil corrupt breeding place of lies and hate and murder; now and mostly it is the ugly unhumorous setting of war, of crumbling houses and broken lives. The Roer is a creek the width of a city avenue, the Rhine is as wide as the Cumberland at Nashville.

The Alps

Kaufbeuren, Bavaria, May 27, 1945: I am living in what was formerly a home for "idiot children."

June 6, 1945: The countryside is all like rolling green velvet, and in the distance the evening sun makes weird, lovely purple and white contrasts in the snowfields of the Alps. Riding along the crest of a hill one loses all sense of proportion as one looks off into the valleys; the little houses and churches are like kindergarten toys made of cardboard. The grazing cows and horses are celluloid miniatures. The churches in the little villages are of three distinct types. There are tiny chapels, some of them perhaps a thousand years old, bare square little buildings without a sign of ornament or architectural distinction except for the inevitable crucifix or altar on the side. There are massive grey stone Romanesque churches from the 12th and 13th centuries; they have been added to over the years, but their simple solid towers reach high up toward the sky with a primitive piety. Then there are the rococo churches, with curving gables and bulbous cupolas and whitewashed facades.

I like the pine trees, and the neat sharp line between the natural meadow-lawns and the curving rim of the forest. The pine trees are so tall that in the midst of the woods only their very tops are full with foliage; the long slender trunks stand bare and flexible, almost like palms. The country is alive with contrasts: desolate bare spaces; fields of tall grass and brush, a few scraggly trees breaking the outline of the horizon. But mainly the rhythm of the landscape is tender and lilting. As I look out of the window now the sky is a streaky wash of bluish-gray, and the trees outside the house etch a delicate intricate indigo pattern against it.

The walls of Kaufbeuren are ringed with an inner walk, and pierced at regular intervals for weapons. The towers set into the walls at the town's four corners might have served as the originals for illustrations in King Arthur books. Their shingles shimmer ruddy and gold in the sunshine. The streets are crooked little alleys, some of them just wide enough for a wagon to pass through, and they bear names like "Lemon Alley," "On the Hill," "Under the Hill." The houses are all old and high, with steep sloping roofs and straight stucco facades. They are colored with every bright hue imaginable: salmon pink, sky blue, lime green, canary yellow, with wonderfully painted shutters and window frames in contrast. After 9 o'clock, when the curfew begins, one can walk down one of these narrow streets and see a curious head at every single window. It gives one the funniest feeling, as though everyone were living like the people in the old-fashioned barometer toy. (Remember the little man who comes smiling out of one door to announce good weather and the little woman who comes scowling out of the other door when it's going to rain?)

This place, of course, hasn't really felt the war as other parts of Germany have, yet its impact lies deep on every aspect of life except the architecture. One sees the war in the empty windows of the stores, in the long queues of women waiting outside food shops, in the hordes of legless and armless German soldiers lolling in the courtyards of the town's many hospitals. Yet withal, I am amazed to realize how close we are to the surrender date when I view the incalculable and unforeseeable steps that have been taken in some directions toward the "return to normalcy."

As I later discovered, there was more to the picture-postcard town of Kaufbeuren than we knew at the time. I later wrote:

July 6, 1945: For the preceding two months I've been with Air PW Interrogation Unit in Wiesbaden, Heidelberg and Kaufbeuren. Our set-up was small and luxurious; the world's most resourceful cook (Spanish, but with a French background) and plenty of slave labor. We lived in a requisitioned building of the Kreis Heilanstalt [County Sanitarium]. It was all most idyllic: lake, lawns, and the sight of the Alps in the distance. Today in the *Stars and Stripes* I learned of what was going on under our noses. I recall my surprise when we first moved into our building (prominently labelled "LUNATIC ASYLUM") to find that it had been a home for feeble-minded children. I remarked at the time that I had thought that the 3rd Reich had no room for such; I was surprised to find them taken care of. One of my colleagues said that the place looked suspicious to him; he thought it was a hideout for SS men disguised as patients. But we never did anything by way of investigation while I was there. The place was a *Vernichtungslager* [extermination camp, and the killings continued even after we were there].[3]

June 6, 1945 [written earlier, while I was still in Kaufbeuren]: While a short month ago the roads were full of freed Russians, Poles and Frenchmen, they are today the thoroughfare for numerous released German soldiers, still wearing Wehrmacht uniforms, with only the swastika insignia and decorations removed. A month ago any alert G.I. would stop any male civilian of military age, to check his papers. Now these same Jerries who were so laboriously herded off to prison camps are headed back home. To the G.I. who is faithful to a woman in the States, or who just wants to keep his nose clean and sticks to the non-fraternization rule, there is something extremely irritating in the sight of a Nazi soldier, in his uniform, walking slowly down the street of an evening in the embrace of a good-looking Fräulein.

Everything is unconscionably peaceful, particularly out in the country, where the normal routine of life, and of diet, is quite unaffected by the occupation. The kids wave, and the appeal "Nix choclit?" is as standard as "Any gum, chum?" was in England. Germany is very very quiet now. This is the lull in which everyone sits tight and waits for the next move. But there will be next moves, I feel sure; there will be eruptions eventually. The Germans are too badly crushed for any revolutionary activity against us to have military significance. But the inner political and social turmoil in Germany will reflect the conflicts and contradictions within the sphere of Allied power, and it is in the resolution of those contradictions that the dangerous possibilities lie.

I'm a soldier in the U.S. Army, am supposed to keep my mouth shut, do my duty, salute my officers and all colors and standards not cased and never allow the foul odor of political inquiry to taint my thoughts (except once a year at election time). All I can say is that I see a lot that the *New York Times* and even *PM* don't run long feature articles about, and I don't like what I know. The most horrible, disillusioning fact of all is that we are falling for the veneer of culture and urbanity (the modern plumbing and the libraries well stocked with Goethe and Schiller) that greets us in the house of the adversary. As I watch the Germans walking the streets and making love and living an increasingly normal life, millions of Russian and Polish Displaced Persons in Germany are confined to barracks pending their transportation home [to Siberian concentration camps, in the case of the Russians, but who knew this in June of 1945?], guarded by American soldiers who are not even permitted to fraternize with them. [The Ukrainians were easily identified by the yellow and blue national flags of the German-imposed separatist regime, which they displayed in the naïve expectation that they were somehow not going back under Soviet rule.]

At Heidelberg we had two young Russian peasant girls who had been slaves in Germany for three years, washing and sewing for the outfit. When we left there we had to return them to the camp [*Lager* in German and Russian]. I won't easily forget how upset they were when I told them. "Oh," said Vera, in a mixture of Russian and German, "How bad, how sad it is in Lager! How unhappy we will be there!"

The Torture Chamber

It was widely rumored, before the war drew to a close, that a hard-core Nazi resistance would be launched from the mountain fastnesses of southern Bavaria. The general staff of the Luftwaffe, along with assorted dignitaries like Hermann Goering and the airplane designer Willy Messerschmidt, were captured in an Alpine redoubt. Goering was immediately shipped elsewhere, but the others were held for preliminary interrogation by a junior lieutenant in our unit. I was supposed to soften them up for him as bad cop to his good cop, except for Messerschmidt, who was given red-carpet treatment by the lieutenant, though he proclaimed his continuing allegiance to Adolf Hitler and his high ideals. The others, mostly colonels and generals, seemed equally unrepentant. What most impressed me was their utterly charmless mediocrity.

What I referred to jokingly as "the torture chamber" was in a suburban villa where the prisoners were held. Unfortunately, I had no racks or wheels at my disposal, but I did have a set of photographs of the stacks of naked corpses in the Dachau concentration camp, which had been taken a short while earlier. To a man, the German officers professed ignorance of the killing installations. They remained complacent when I tried to make them quaver by pointing to the pictures and saying sternly, *"Dass haben* Sie *getan!"* (*You* did this!)

The most compliant creature of the lot was an SS general, who stood at rigid attention when I, a mere staff sergeant, addressed him. He had a brutal pockmarked face and eyes like pale tinted glass beads. Not only did he know nothing about concentration camps; he was merely a simple policeman who was doing his honorable duty. (Within a few hours he had shed the insignia of rank and of the SS from his uniform.) I had a strong temptation to take him outside and shoot him while he "escaped," but the impulse to conduct such a cold-blooded execution was at odds with my nature, and I let him live.

My best shot at unnerving the prisoners was to have them strip to check for hidden weapons or poison pills of the kind that some of the Nazi big shots like Himmler had already taken (and which Goering took also, before his scheduled execution). A colonel with high tight-fitting boots protested that he could not remove them himself, so I delegated a seething boyish-looking blond major to act as his orderly.

A British intelligence officer attached to our unit described, but did not actually provide a live demonstration of, his preferred method for extracting information from captured enemies. In the peremptory manner of a Prussian drill sergeant, he first called the prisoner to attention and then repeatedly ordered him to kneel. *("Knicksen!!")* Apparently compliance always followed.

Among the Russians who had attached themselves to us was a large unkempt Red Army man whom I addressed solemnly, with my winking eye turned away from the Germans. *"Sovietskiy Kommissar uzhe nye priyechal?"* (The Soviet commissar hasn't come yet?") He fell in with the gag and shook his head. *"Uzhe nyet"* ("not yet").

Having thus cruelly softened up the prisoners, I escorted them one by one to the room where the lieutenant sat, and he smiled broadly, extended his hand with feigned cordiality, and began his debriefing.

A day or so later, while our prisoners awaited their fate, another army intelligence officer arrived, bringing a new bag of tricks. His principal tool was a recently invented wire recorder, and his mission was to eavesdrop surreptitiously on the conversations the Germans were having among themselves. What better place to do this than in the dining room of our villa? He installed his equipment in the room immediately above it, drilled a hole through the floor, and hid a small microphone in the dining room's ceiling light fixture. When we tested this brilliant device, speech turned out to be unintelligible, because voices rattled back and forth in the bare room. It was clear that the acoustics had to be improved. From elsewhere in the spacious house we brought in rugs, pictures and furniture. Though this improved our reception, the staff officers were not taken in by this effort to provide them with more luxurious mealtime accommodations. Their conversations were entirely innocuous, but every once in a while there was a "ssssh" or a throat clearing, followed by silence. Whatever secrets they possessed, they were not about to share with us, inadvertently or otherwise.

Dreyfus and Leeds

At this location, those of us who had come from Flap Dog were joined by some familiar faces. Among them were two deadly antagonists who had first met and battled on the tennis courts at Vanderbilt. Perhaps their mutual antipathy rested on their physical resemblance; both had the features and some of the priapic instincts of a satyr. Both also had somewhat privileged origins, and both were quick to anger. Blond, perpetually sunbronzed Werner Dreyfus, a grandnephew of the famous Capt. Alfred Dreyfus, came from Mulhouse, and spoke French and German with equal facility. He had been in the United States four years. (Dreyfus had visited the newly freed Buchenwald concentration camp and had taken the photographs that I used in my futile efforts to intimidate the captive German officers.)[4]

Dark-haired Julius Schwarz had left his parents in Hamburg and had since learned that they had met the usual fate of European Jews. While in Nashville, he had legally changed his name to Franklin T. (presumably standing for "Telano") Leeds. In freshly occupied Germany, Leeds felt unrestrained by the usual code of civil conduct. He enjoyed careening about in a jeep, missing German pedestrians by a hair's breadth and laughing hilariously. When I chided him after a near-miss with one black-dressed old lady, he said, "The Nazis killed my mother and father. So what if I give them a good scare!"

Leeds and I took part in a curious project. We were to search for the Luftwaffe's top pilots, especially those of the new jet fighter planes, and recruit them to teach their tricks to the American air force. To round them up we had to go to the massive enclosures, ringed by barbed wire, in which thousands and thousands of newly surrendered German troops were being held, officers separate from the enlisted men. They milled around chatting, with no diversion except meals.

Leeds and I entered different compounds separately in search of specific individuals. Naïvely, I went in with my carbine over my shoulder where any prisoner could have grabbed it, held me hostage, or done me in. But this was a defeated and disoriented horde who looked at me without interest. There was one exception: I was approached by a member of Vlasov's army, who wanted a private conversation, which we conducted half in German, half in Russian. He was, he said, a Jew, a captured soldier in the Red Army who had disguised his identity and served with the renegade force rather than confront the precarious prospects of slave labor as an ordinary prisoner. He had lived for three years in peril of being found out. Now what was to happen to him? He looked Jewish and spoke Yiddish, so I took his story to be true and explained it to the MPs in charge of the compound. But as in so many fascinating but momentary encounters, I never learned what happened afterwards.

Another prisoner who wanted special treatment was a fellow who spoke impeccable American English. He had in fact spent most of his life in the States but had returned to Germany just before the start of the war to attend the University of Kiel. He claimed to have been drafted into the Wehrmacht against his will, but I assumed that he had gone back to the Fatherland in order to share in the glory of its military conquests. He had spent the war doing intelligence work. What I considered to be his treason evoked no sympathy from me, but undoubtedly other Americans must have been taken in by the innocent manner in which he told his story.

The dozen or so of the Luftwaffe's aces whom we pulled out of the prison compounds were a younger but more impressive bunch than their superiors on the general staff. Theirs were some of the radio voices to which we had been listening for the past eight months. Leeds initiated our individual conversations with them by asking them about their achievements. *"Wie viele Abschüsse?"* ("How many planes have you shot down?") The answers were astonishing: 36, 104, 65, and so forth. Most of these had been on the Eastern front. Leeds continued by saying, "We're continuing the war against Japan. Would you like to help us?" To a man they jumped at the opportunity to turn against their former partners, I think with the illusion that we were about to put them back in their fighter planes and ship them to the Pacific for further battles. Whatever their fantasies, I couldn't fault them for wanting to get out of the camp and go somewhere, anywhere. So we loaded them into a truck and took them on a long ride to a big house in Heidelberg, which had come through the war unscathed. The streets were full of comfortable-looking civilians, and the traffic, civilian and military, was being directed by German policemen. The pilots were astonished at this display of normalcy. "*Deutsche Polizei* [German police]?" one asked me. "*Natürlich*," I replied. Their initial surliness quickly dissipated.

They reappeared after showering, without the beards that some of them had started in the last few weeks of captivity. One announced jovially that he was ready to find himself *"ein Frauenpelz"* (some pussy), though that opportunity did not immediately present itself to any of them. Although they had spearheaded Hitler's war, their activities seemed to lack any trace of ideological motivation. They glumly acknowledged, when I put it to them, that many of Germany's best writers, artists, scientists, and intellectuals had fled abroad, but the politics of the Nazi dictatorship seemed utterly irrelevant to them.

Incidental Dramas

In pursuit of our mission we drove back and forth across the Bavarian countryside, in endless streams of military traffic crawling along detours around the destroyed viaducts of the Autobahn. We gawked at Hitler's Wolf's Lair at Berchtesgaden.

Berchtesgaden, June 8, 1945: I'm here at Hitler's former mountain hideout on a short business trip through the German and Austrian Tyrol. I have never before seen a landscape as impressive as that of the Alps, with their jagged gray granite crests, snow-covered and towering over the rolling green valleys. No matter which way one turns, the scene is always like a picture postcard, with the colors fantastically pure and bright and the contrasts of depth and height spectacular. One sees no sign of the war as one rides through the peaceful little villages.

In Helmstedt, I wandered through the empty zoological garden, a late-nineteenth-century folly with richly ornamented green-painted wrought-iron cages. Except for some odd creatures—birds, armadillos, and reptiles—the animals had been eaten or had died of hunger.

Munich, June 12, 1945: Munich is pretty badly chewed up. Both Pinakotheken [the art museums] are destroyed. The trolleys are running, though, with their windows boarded up.

Most of the members of my team were European refugees who had served in military intelligence with the ground forces during the campaign. One of them was a half-Jewish corporal, originally from Mainz, whose sister had remained behind in Germany with her husband, who had been called up for the army. He was determined to find her, and I accompanied him on a side-trip to her last-known address, which turned out to be a modest suburban house in a small bombed-out city in central Germany. We were in a hurry, and his reunion was brief and emotional. His brother-in-law, it turned out, was a prisoner of the Russians. These glorious spring days were full of such minor dramas, in which I was witness to a passing moment without ever seeing the plot unfold.

A beer garden in Heidelberg had been commandeered for the American troops. The waitresses were exchanging banter cheerfully with the soldiers, in spite of the non-fraternization rules that forbade such contacts. The young women were evidently not Germans, but D.P.'s (Displaced Persons—the euphemism applied to all those foreigners who had been enslaved in Germany in one way or another). When we addressed one of them it turned out that they were among the few fortunate Polish Jews who had survived as factory slave workers in Germany. One of my companions in uniform was a Polish Jew who had lived in Austria and who had managed to get to America on the eve of the war. He and I had often discussed the disasters of Europe. Eagerly, he asked the girl in Yiddish where she was from and remarked that he had family in a nearby town. "And do you happen to know what happened to them?" She gave him a long, shocked look. "Don't you know?" she finally asked. "Don't you know?" My companion collapsed in convulsive sobs. Of course he had known, but he had not yet known with certainty and finality.

The same companion was adept at finding treasures in the midst of the captured document files through which we were asked to sift. There was one sheaf of handwritten correspondence from an SS officer at the Eastern Front, who wrote, *"Man fühlt sich den Leuten so überlegen!"* ("One feels so superior to these people!") My friend shook his head sadly. "This is a grown man, writing like this?"

It was either he or I who disposed of a remarkable letter addressed to the supreme allied commander from Aachen even before the Battle of the Bulge:

XXX Metal Works
Metal Works for All Branches of Industry
Raw and Processed

December 1, 1944

Supreme General Eisenhower
Highly Personal
The Nazis have done me every possible injury!
Now I have built a motor that runs on water.

To produce energy it requires *no oil! no gasoline! no steam! Only cold water!*

Oil and coal are not needed to produce energy. When the machine stands in water it runs by *itself* and produces electrical current in limitless quantities. This model was destroyed in a bombing raid.

General Eisenhower, send me to America, to your President Roosevelt, so that this discovery is not lost. Through this machine Mr. Roosevelt will have the oil and coal syndicates in his hands. This discovery is not good for the Hitlers.

General, make a gift of this invention to your glorious America, which has freed us from the terror.

This is my thanks for being allowed to return to my house.

Nancy

My travels in Germany came to an abrupt end.

Nancy, France, July 6, 1945: This finds me in a veritable hotbed of 65th Infantry Division riflemen, all in variously battered condition (mostly from playing baseball.) *Quant à moi* (as for me), my injury was strictly business. On June 8, while on a field trip to Berchtesgaden and the Tyrol, I was taking a Kraut to the PWE (prisoner of war enclosure), my weapons carrier skidded and we all rolled over and over down an Alp.

The "Kraut" was the Luftwaffe's principal expert on the Soviet air force, a former pilot who had lost an arm but remained on duty as an intelligence officer. Along with a Capt. Curtis Davis from Baltimore (who became a historian in later life), I went to track him down at home. As we headed back toward town, we were caught in a sudden downpour. Davis had a cocktail date and was anxious to get back quickly, so instead of pulling over and waiting for the shower to pass, he insisted on driving in the uncovered front of the truck, while I joined the prisoner in the back and kept dry. The truck, by the way, had a name: Jumbo. By the time we got to Berchtesgaden, the rain had stopped, but Davis was thoroughly drenched. He ordered me to take the prisoner to the compound, which was some distance away. I had never before driven a half-ton truck, whose mechanism was more complex than that of the jeep, to which I was just getting accustomed. When I went into a skid on a turn of the winding road, I tried unsuccessfully to brake and was faced with a towering cliff ahead of me or a free fall down the mountain. As the truck fell front over end I was thrown clear; army vehicles had no seat belts.

For a moment I thought I knew what man's final mortal sensations are. Life hasn't been pleasant since then. The Kraut, who had only one arm to start out with, got off with bruises and was solicitously tended by the *Zivilbevölkerung* [the civilian population]. He kept muttering, *"Der arme Jumbo!"* ["Poor Jumbo!"]

My left elbow was bashed up. "A sprain," said the 101st Airborne medics, and with our business done and a receipt for one (1) weapons carrier in the Captain's pocket, we headed back up the Autobahn to Kaufbeuren. More X-rays and diagnoses, a plane ride here to Nancy. The surgeon tells me my elbow is "about as bad as an elbow can be." Operation: four hours on the cutting table, penicillin jabs every three hours day and night for a week. The lousy part is that I'll probably never have full use of my arm again. Until the sutures were removed I was confined to bed with my arm slung up with pulleys and weights.

"States" as such has no overwhelming attraction for me now. Life in Germany is much more comfortable and interesting.

Conversation with the French nurse's aides in the hospital ward centered on the subject of *zig-zig* **(sex). One poor woman who had taken an American sergeant as her lover was teased mercilessly from morning to night as she went about administering back-rubs and dispensing good cheer. There was a vigorous trade in cigarettes through the open windows. And there were endless card games. With my arm in a cast and a sling, I was permitted to go out on a day pass and resume my passionate sightseeing.**

July 23, 1945: Toul had been partly destroyed by the *furor germanicus* in 1940. The old Gothic cathedral had one tower ruined, and the interior, which had been swept by fire, was boarded up. It's amazing to see how much France looks like its pictures, as painted by its many great artists. Every place one comes to gives one the feeling that one has seen it before. I sat for a while in a café watching the confusion attending the departure of a bus for a town about 100 miles away. There were about four times as many people wanting to get on as there was actually room for, and about 50 of them managed somehow to get on. Those who just couldn't fit inside scrambled on top of the roof and balanced themselves amidst the load of bicycles and suitcases that were already there.

At the railroad station in Toul, a small elderly woman dressed in black awaited the arrival of a slow-moving local train. Among the passengers who got off was her son, a former war prisoner still dressed in the incongruous light-blue uniform that French troops had worn before the debacle of 1940. They said nothing but embraced each other very, very tightly and then walked down the street.

August 5, 1945: Yesterday I went out to the country with two friends, up along the valley of the Moselle. You'd think that among all those farms it would be an easy job getting something to eat, but we had a terrific time finding some eggs, which we ate fried, some French bread and very sweet little plums (mirabelles, they're called) all washed down with vin rouge and beer. There's been hardly any rain this year and the crops are all drying and dying in the fields. It's not a good thing for the hungry people of Europe.

August 9, 1945: As for my postwar plans; I'm pretty sure I'll do some graduate work but I'm positive it won't be in the field of law [my father's original profession, which he had urged me to pursue]. The practice of law in the U.S. is completely tied up with the corruptness, crookedness and villainy of business for "profit," which I hate with all my heart.

August 18, 1945: While the war has been slowly ending in a series of epileptic anti-climaxes, the past few days have brought similarly muted crisis to our ward. Our doctor, who has been too much overworked or too lazy to get our records in order during the last few months, has departed on leave to the Riviera, and in a flurry of effort and self-sacrifice, disposed of our histories the night before he left. (One of our Italian co-belligerents has just entered the Red Cross facility, bestowing a friendly Fascist salute to other co-belligerents, who are playing pool.[5]) What this means is that after a further period of agonized suspense I shall probably be sent to a general hospital, Z.I.

Having explored all the high life and low life of Nancy I have recently begun to devote my pass afternoons to excursions, to Metz (where the stately République Française publishes bilingual proclamations), Pont à Mousson with its idle mills, Lunéville of the fine baroque church and mouldering barracks.

I really like France. I like almost everywhere I go in Europe, because the houses are always built to be lived in and not because there was profit to be made from their construction. But I haven't yet found a single G.I. who likes this country and its people, who doesn't make bitter comparisons with the paradise of Germany whose buildings have good plumbing "just like in the States" and whose women fuck with joy and inspiration for a chocolate bar, yet are not whores like the French girls.

The sordid inertia of these last two months has done much to mar my formerly bouncing humanism. Maybe it's less the lack of new and vital experience and companionship than it is the inevitable hospital introspection. The unexpectedly sudden end of the war points up more critically than before my utter unpreparedness to resume where I left off in civilian life. I should set about acquiring a secure and thorough background in some professional field other than the nebulous one of "contempry liture." But what? There's much that interests me, yet nothing at this stage that overwhelmingly absorbs me. I still can't think of anything more worthy of effort than to write about the world and its people in such a way that ideas are set in motion by the story. I'll never be really happy in any work which is devoid of positive and progressive political implications. I'll never be an activist, but any job which involves people and ideas is in some measure a "political" one.

We listened on the radio to Harry Truman describing the atomic bomb; his speech left me awed and somehow disheartened at the thought of the demons he had unleashed. V-J Day (September 2, 1945) occasioned great celebration.

Naturally my first reaction on hearing of the Japanese surrender was one of unrestrained joy that the loyal East Indians will at last be returned to their beloved Queen. *"Indie moet vrij!"* ["The East Indies must be free!"] said the posters in Maastricht last winter. *"Engagez-vous pour delivrer l'Indochine!"* ["Enlist to free Indochina!"] read the posters in Nancy now.[6]

The Return

I was flown to the states in a hospital DC-3 outfitted with stacks of litters. Although I was perfectly ambulatory, as the expression went, I had to spend the entire long flight on my back, except for brief refueling stops in the Azores and at Gander. When I arrived at Rhoads General Hospital in Utica, New York, the physical therapists encouraged me to exercise my frozen elbow and I did this compulsively in the hope that I would recover its use (which I never did). But on a trip to New York, I was told by a kindly Park Avenue orthopedist that my arm required complete rest.

Soon afterwards, the army medics decided that they had done all they could for me and were set to discharge me. This final step required a routine physical examination. Now came another complication: A chest X-ray showed a spot on my lung, which was interpreted as a possible sign of tuberculosis. To find out whether the lesion was active, or merely the residue of a then-common infantile illness, the X-ray would have to be compared with the one taken at the time of my induction into the army. But in the meanwhile, no chances could be taken.

January 24, 1946: This morning I went down to the office to see if I could go on pass this weekend. They told me that I was leaving for North Carolina tonight on a special troop train. I'm inured by now to the abrupt beginnings of all Army transportation. It doesn't seem as though there's anything left to be said or done except to pack and get ready for the vague strange things that are about to happen to me.

I was dispatched to the tuberculosis ward of Moore General Hospital at Swannanoa in the Black Mountains of western North Carolina.

January 28, 1946: I came down here in a characteristically fucked-up G.I. troop movement which gave me no time at home, although we were in NY for 8 hours and shuttled around the Washington railroad yards for another four.

It's the old Army game. I've been here three days and no doctor has yet appeared. We are confined to our ward and are required to lie in our beds day and night. There are three amplifiers playing the hospital programs and seven privately owned radios, all of which blare constant streams of poisonous idiocy and degradation. It is utterly impossible to read even the simplest and lightest fiction in the midst of this frenzied din. (I am able to write this only by escaping to the sun porch.) If I can't be assigned to a private room as a T.B. patient I shall turn myself in as a psycho and ask for a padded cell. (Question on a quiz program today: "Now think hard. After what state is Lake Michigan named?")

The physician in charge of our ward, Captain La Verne, admonished us to banish litter from our night tables and reminded us repeatedly that "cleanliness is next to Godliness."

At that time TB was treated with bed rest and a high fat diet. I drank several quarts of milk each day, stayed in bed and gained nearly forty pounds. Eventually I was taken off bed rest, and went off on excursions to the Greensboro home of Thomas Wolfe, to Black Mountain College (at the peak of its short interesting life), and to the Great Smoky Mountains and the dams and lakes of the Tennessee Valley Authority.

At the army camp to which the hospital was attached, sunburned, healthy-looking German prisoners taken in North Africa marched back and forth in close order formation, singing nostalgically, *"Ach, die Vögelein in der Heimat, Sie singen so wunder- wunderschön! In der Heimat, in der Heimat, da gibt's ein Wiedersehen!"* ["Oh the birdies in the homeland, they sing so beauti- beautifully! In the homeland, in the homeland, there'll be a get-together!"]

It was at Moore that a southern buck sergeant showed me a letter and asked, "Sergeant, that's nigger writing, ain't it?" I had to assure him, with a blank face, that there was no way to tell.

Among the white southerners whom I encountered on hospital wards there were several who were distinguished both by an extraordinary capacity for comedy and by an unquenchable delight in bigotry. There was one nonstop talker whose target shifted from contemptuous ejaculations of "New York!" or "Brooklyn!" to "damn niggers!" Yet his most outrageous utterances were laced with devastating wit.

In retrospect, it is amazing how little vulgar language was used in the army of those days. The southerners' expletive, "She-yut!" ("Shit!") was common, but I never heard the term "motherfucker" until I went to Korea in 1951.

There's an amplifier howling at thousands of decibels, to which no one is listening except our stolid illiterate ward Indian. Most of what's wrong here is what's wrong with the Army in general. [I had decided to become a sociologist, and the passage of the G.I. Bill made it possible for me to go to graduate school when I left the service.] I am studying criminology and abnormal psych and rural sociology and statistical analysis in USAFI [Armed Forces Institute correspondence] courses and there are the odds and ends of correspondence and occasional lighter reading or shit-shooting to fill in the time. I've even learned to play casino and hearts. But there's a definite Gresham's Law in Army social life. The common denominator of taste and manners and courtesy is always established by the lowest element.

The thing that upsets and obsesses me most is that time and events are passing me by.

Swannanoa, May, 1946: Fired by all my reading about labor unions I decided to hitchhike to Gastonia to see where all the trouble started, but I left here too late and my voyage degenerated into a purposeless jaunt through the North Carolina countryside.[7] The rural housing hereabouts is unspeakably primitive, though after all my Southern voyages I no longer have any right to be shocked. The mountain folk sprawl in the doorways of their log shacks and spit tobacco juice at the sun.

The other day I visited Linville Caverns, where a guide singsongs a prefabricated story about the stalactites and stalagmites and orders us to "use our imagination" to convert them into Franciscan monks, lambs, elephants' ears, catfish and heads of Abraham Lincoln. Despite all the blatant commercialization, these mountains still manage to subdue all human encroachments. They're always changing with the weather and the time of day. In the early evening of a sunny day each tree is separately delineated in a warm clear light and the ridges stretch on for row upon row until the ultimate vague blue ridge on the horizon. But on a rainy day one can see only the nearest hills, turned a neutral photographic, and the fog banks roll gracefully up their slopes and disappear.

Amidst all this rusticity, Black Mountain College strangely obtrudes its little citadel of culture.[8] [I attended a concert by] a quartet playing Mozart and Beethoven. The girls wore evening gowns, with bare feet in sandals.

My ward neighbors include a pleasant boy from Mississippi who writes a daily letter to his Mommy and a great hulking youth from Brooklyn who has not changed his socks or underwear in the three months he's been here. Sunday here is always enlivened by a large blond proletarian from California who was overseas for 4+ years, He imbibes heavily of the poisonous green potion known as "Mountain Dew" which is widely bootlegged hereabouts and then goes roaring up and down the ward, "Fuck John L. Lewis!"[9]

One of those episodes to which one never becomes inured no matter how frequently they occur: Lee is a Negro fellow, a New Yorker, about 35, with a little girl of seven. He is a pleasant talkative chap returned from service with a Tank Destroyer outfit in Europe. He tells us that he has never run into any trouble in the Army. Saturday he received a telegram telling him that his grandmother had died. He went into Asheville to call home and attend to some business, had nothing to drink, and at 12:30 was sitting in the "colored" section of the Jim Crow station waiting for the bus back to camp. Two white M.P.s entered—both Southerners, both rookies of 18 with only a few months' service in the Army. They asked for his pass, which was in order. Two other Negro soldiers sitting in the waiting room got up and walked out. Perhaps they had no passes. The M.P.s followed them but returned a few minutes later with two M.P. sergeants. One said to Lee, "You're coming down to the police station with us." "Why?" said Lee. In answer he was slapped in the face. He was then dragged outside by the four M.P.s. Two held his arms and the other two beat him savagely on the face and body with their truncheons, so savagely that X-rays had to be taken when he got to the hospital. His shirt and tie were ripped. A crowd of about fifty civilians (white) gathered about and urged the M.P.s to "Hit him in the balls!" Lee offered no resistance, except to say he didn't want to go the police station and to remind the M.P.s that he was a hospital patient. A number of white soldiers stood by and made no move to intercede until fortunately one of the men on our ward happened to be attracted by the crowd and offered to ride with Lee to the police station, from which he was taken to the guard house here. He was released the next morning but he looks pitiable and says, "Them M.P.s are just itching to use their clubs on a colored fellow."

Swannanoa, May 16, 1946: The latest news flash from the Moore front is as disconcerting as usual. My induction X-ray film has been lost. Naturally no one except myself has the slightest interest in finding it and I can't look for it, nor can I be discharged without it. After eight days here I finally got to see the doctor, who began by cheerfully reneging on this former promises to let me out immediately (the "rules" were changed while I was gone). My time here is not devoted to medical treatment of any kind, but simply to hanging around waiting for someone to shuffle my papers up. Is not mine a righteous bitterness?

My induction X-ray finally appeared from the Pentagon archives, four months after it had been requested.

May 21, 1946: I saw the doctor. He said it was too bad about my X-ray films being lost, and that he chose to accept the reading given here—which was that I had a TB spot on my lung when I was inducted, should therefore never have been in the Army, that I have a completely arrested case since there has been no change in four years, that all this period of hospitalization was completely unnecessary. If my induction film had not through error been sent back to Washington from Rhoads I would have been discharged immediately on arriving here.

A few days later I received my final pay, a voucher for travel back to New York, a certificate of honorable discharge, and a small gilt lapel pin to be worn on my civilian jacket. The pin bore the stylized head of an eagle, but it was universally referred to as "the ruptured duck."

Afterword

Some of the letters in this volume were sent to my parents, and kept by my doting mother (though she threw out my Nazi memorabilia, including a number of gold medals whose metal may well have originated in the teeth fillings and wedding rings of murdered Jews). Other letters were written to a girl with whom I had an intense romance during my stay at Vanderbilt University. She returned them to me, with what was known as a "Dear John" letter, while I was in the hospital after the war's end. The rest of the letters were written to my best friend, who had entered the army shortly before me. Before I shipped overseas, I asked him to visit my girlfriend. They eloped at the war's end and I never saw either of them again. After his death in 1996, his widow discovered that he had kept my letters through the following half century, and she sent them back to me. Before she disappeared from view in 1946, she had suggested that I look up Agnes, a fellow-organizer in the South for the Textile Workers Union, to whom I have been married since 1948. All this, however, is another story.

Notes

Preface

1. "Fewer than l million, probably no more than 800,000, took any part in extended combat. In numerous theaters [of war] fighting men comprised 10 per cent, or less, of the full military complement." Gerald Linderman, *The World within War: America's Combat Experience in World War II* (New York: Free Press, 1997), p. 1. Not all casualties occurred in combat, but Linderman's estimates are hard to reconcile with the offical figures of over 400,000 killed and a million wounded. In 1945 an infantry division with a complement of 14,000 men (including artillery, engineer, signal, quartermaster, medical, and headquarters units as well as riflemen) was supported by over 66,500 troops in the zone of operations and in the United States—a ratio of one to five. (U.S. Army Office of the Chief Military Historian, "The Division Slice and the Division Force," Project 38, February, 1964.)
2. I studied French and Latin in high school and Spanish in college.

Chapter 1. Preliminaries

1. But they were not. See John Horne and Alan Kramer, *German Atrocities, 1914: A History of Denial* (New Haven: Yale University Press, 2001).
2. Yorkville is a neighborhood on Manhattan's upper east side, which then had a large German population and was the headquarters of the Nazi German-American Bund.
3. Exact dates are missing from many of the letters transcribed here. I sometimes headed them by the day of the week.
4. This was an annual event in New York. In the 1930s it had wide participation from labor unions and a variety of left-wing organizations, among which the Communists took an increasing lead.
5. The German code name for the invasion of the Soviet Union.
6. Beniamino Gigli, the great Italian tenor, a favorite of Mussolini's.
7. Thompson was a widely syndicated newspaper columnist, wife of the novelist Sinclair Lewis and a friend of Leo Balet.
8. Brown was a British journalist.

Chapter 3. Military Academia

1. The United Service Organization had set up servicemen's clubs in major cities and in towns near military installations. They offered coffee and doughnuts, reading matter, game facilities, and dances.
2. "Soldier Thinking," Sept. 27, 1943.
3. Rhoda Jaffe Klonsky began an affair with W. H. Auden in the spring of 1946, after he and Kallman had agreed to suspend sexual relations.

Chapter 4. Preparing to Go Over There

1. The term *Wehrmacht* covers the entire German military, but was generally used to refer to the army.
2. The Federal Communications Commission had set up this service to listen to and digest enemy and other foreign broadcasts for intelligence gathering.
3. The ASTP had been drastically reduced in February, 1944, with 73,000 of its troops assigned to the army's ground forces, primarily the infantry. They suffered substantial casualties when they were sent in as replacement troops during the Battle of the Bulge. A number of reassigned ASTP men have recently written memoirs detailing the shock of this shift from the university to the battlefield. Robert Kotlowitz, *Before Their Time: A Memoir* (New York: Knopf, 1997); A. Cleveland Harrison, *Unsung Valor: A GI's Story of World War II* (Jackson: University Press of Mississippi, 2000); George W. Neill, *Infantry Soldier: Holding the Line at the Battle of the Bulge* (Norman: University of Oklahoma Press, 2000); Leon Standifer, *Not in Vain: A Rifleman Remembers World War II* (Baton Rouge: Louisiana State University Press, 1992); Bruce Egger and Lee M. Otts (not an ASTPer), *G Company's War: Two Personal Accounts of the Campaigns in Europe, 1944–45* (Tuscaloosa: University of Alabama Press, 1992.) All of these men served in Europe and most of them subsequently entered academic careers. Another author was sent to the Pacific: Frank Furlong Mathias, *G.I. Jive: An Army Bandsman in World War II* (Lexington: University of Kentucky Press, 1982).
4. Pepper ended his career as a congressman.

Chapter 5. The Theater of War

1. In reference to this chapter's title, the term "Theater of Operations" applies to a whole sphere of military activity. Britain was part of the European Theater of Operations (the E.T.O.). The continental United States constituted the Zone of the Interior (the Z.I.).
2. It was memorialized in George Orwell's book, *The Road to Wigan Pier* (London: Secker and Warburg, 1986).
3. The words of a popular song of the time, whose title in Spanish has an ambiguous meaning.
4. This sacrifice was apparently in vain. "Efforts to extend the range and value of Y (radio) intelligence by including airborne operators in bomber formations proved of limited tactical value. . . . Operators were present on only a few bombers. They could provide immediate warning information only to their own crew, since radio silence precluded broadcasting over radio frequencies" (John F. Kreis, ed., *Piercing the Fog: Intelligence and Army Air Force Operations in World War II* [Washington, D.C.: Air Force History and Museum Program, 1996], p. 97).
5. I did not bring up this subject when I met von Braun many years later. He was by then an honored leader of America's space program.
6. "Dog" stood for the letter D in the Army's phonetic alphabet, used to avoid confusion in telephone and radio communication.
7. An advance unit of the squadron had begun operations on the continent three days after the Normandy landings. "At each fighter control center the Y (signal intelligence) officer sat beside the chief controller. This arrangement allowed for the immediate operational application of time-sensitive Y information, since the chief controller was in direct contact with airborne aircraft as well as with the appropriate tactical air control headquarters." Kreis, *Piercing the Fog*, p. 98.

Chapter 6. On the Continent

1. *Das Reich* was a glossy Nazi newspaper aimed at Germany's intellectual elite.
2. The national police force set up by the collaborationist French regime in Vichy.

Chapter 7. On the Heels of the Wehrmacht

1. This might be the equivalent of $10 today.
2. Luxembourg had been absorbed by the Third Reich, its men drafted into the Wehrmacht, and its institutions incorporated into their German counterparts. Although the little country's official language was and is French, its inhabitants speak a Germanic patois.

Chapter 8. The Chateau

1. The Battle of the Bulge, or the von Rundstedt offensive, also known as the battle of the Ardennes, sought to break through the Allied lines and recapture the all-important port of Antwerp.

Chapter 9. The Discovery of Germany

1. St. Lo is a town in Normandy that was pivotal in the Allied breakout from the original beachhead after the invasion.
2. A Gauleiter was the regional Nazi autocrat.
   The Volkssturm was the reserve of older men and teenagers created to bolster the Wehrmacht's manpower in the Third Reich's final months.
3. As it turned out, this dire forecast was not too far from what actually happened.
4. Ernst Thälmann was the prewar leader of the German Communist Party.
5. Strotz described his return visit in a letter to his mother, dated February 26: "Bomb craters, the remnants of an airplane which had crashed, the tracks of the American tanks which had manoeuvred in the meadow, the fence posts captioned with German helmets and the hat of a civilian who purportedly had been accused of sabotage because he carried an American flashlight battery. . . . The 2000 Germans in Bondorf gave all the homes a terrific ransacking, devouring all the food supplies, all the wine, breaking dishes, burning books, wrecking sewing machines, smashing radios, stealing bedding and using sheets for camouflage. Goodly numbers were paratroopers, soldiers dressed in American uniforms, teen-age kids, and, believe it or not, Blitzmädel. But most remarkable is that some sixty *'Lustfrauen'* [prostitutes] were captured by the Americans, the German troops having brought them not simply up behind the front, but directly into the front, into the very battle! . . . Two civilians from another village had been brought along as prisoners by the Germans. They were made to dig their own graves, then shot."
6. Rosenberg was a leading exponent of Nazi racial doctrine who put his theories into practice in the brutal occupation of the Ukraine.
7. Literally, Hail Mealtime. This was a fiction, invented to cover up the Hitler greeting into which he was automatically propelled at the sight of higher authority.

Chapter 10. A Postwar Assignment

1. This had already happened when I next visited Wiesbaden in 1952.
2. Yoselowitz, a member of the original Vanderbilt ASTP contingent, was among those assigned for flying duty with the Eighth Air Force. His plane was shot down, he parachuted, was beaten by his civilian captors, but ended in a prison compound. Fortunately, he was not among the many American Jewish war prisoners who were worked and starved to death in the mines of Saxony.
3. The army newspaper *Stars and Stripes* reported on July 5, 1945, that a nurse at the Kaufbeuren installation "said the last child she killed . . . was murdered on May 29, 33 days after American troops took the town. . . . Captured correspondence [sic] indicated that the Kaufbeuren and Irsee asylums were used as human warehouses from which German scientists needing human beings for experiments in other fields could draw at will. . . . The murder factory at Kaufbeuren was no secret to the people in the community. One 12-year old urchin in the town when asked to identify a building replied casually, 'Oh, that's where they kill them.'" "A law of July 14, 1933, led first to the sterilization, and then to the killing, mostly by gas, of at least 70,000 Germans because they were retarded, mentally ill, crippled, or otherwise seen as defective." (Istvan Deak, "The Crime of the Century," *New York Review of Books*, Sept. 26, 2002, pp. 48–51.)
4. Alfred Dreyfus, the victim of an anti-Semitic conspiracy, was sentenced to imprisonment on Devil's Island. He was pardoned and eventually exonerated after a vigorous campaign led by the novelist Émile Zola. The sharp political divisions aroused by the Dreyfus case persist in France after more than a century.
5. The Italians, formerly enemies, had been redesignated "co-belligerents" after they switched

sides in the wake of the Allied invasion of Southern Italy. The Italian prisoners of war were subsequently treated differently than the Germans.
6. My sarcastic tone was well-warranted. The Allies' agreement to let the French resume control of Indochina was the inevitable precursor to the Vietnam War.
7. Gastonia was the site of a famous and bloody textile workers' strike.
8. Black Mountain College was an experimental college dedicated to the arts, which lasted from 1933 to 1956.
9. Lewis was the head of both the United Mine Workers and the Congress of Industrial Organizations.

Index

Aachen, 48, 88, 78–79, 93
Accident, 133
Acuff, Roy, 30–31
AGCT. *See* Army General Classification Test
American League Against War and Fascism, 4
American Youth for Democracy, 40
Amtorg, 7
Anti-Nazis, German. *See* German anti-Nazis
Anti-Semitism, 33, 47, 82
Aristocracy, Belgian, 74
Arlon, 65–67
Armed Forces Radio Network, 59
Army General Classification Test, 23
Army Specialized Training Program, xv, 20, 23, 37, 53, 55, 143n
ASTP. *See* Army Specialized Training Program
Atlantic crossing. *See* Queen Mary
Atrocities, Nazi, 4, 65–66, 68, 69, 72, 79, 88, 104, 106, 110, 113, 116, 125–26, 128, 132, 145n
Auden, Wystan H., 10, 143n
Axelrod, Sidney, 58, 77, 79

Balet, Leo, 6, 32–33, 37, 143n
Band practice, 16
Baroness, at Fouron St. Pierre, 74–76, 83
Basic Training, 13–25
Bastogne, 73, 86
Battle of the Bulge, 144n
Belov, Fyodor I., 7, 11
Berchtesgaden, 131
Bielefeld, 97–98
Black Mountain College, 137, 138, 146n
Bombing, effects of, 89, 94, 123
Bondorf, Luxembourg, 67–69
Bougival, 63–64
Brand, Oscar, 33, 79, 83
Brauer, Max, 31
Braun, Wernher von, 144n
Brooklyn College, 3, 4, 40
Bureaucracy, military, xiv
Buzz Bombs. *See* V-1 Rockets

Camp Crowder, 17–25
Canterbury, 56
Carlson, Robert O., 27–28
Carthage, Missouri, 19–20
Censorship, 88
Chateau de la Commanderie, 73–78
Chermayeff, Serge, 33; visit to relatives, 83–84
Children, reaction to soldiers, 61, 63, 68, 70, 91
Chorley, Lancashire, 49–52
Cologne, 93, 95–96
Combat, xiii
Communists, 4; American and Russian compared, 11, 12; German, 105, 115
Concentration camps, 106, 128
Cornell, Katherine, 78
C Rations, 62
Cream, Joe, 24
Cryptanalysis, 35, 94

Davis, Curtis, 133
D-Day, 39–40, 60
Dinant, 83–84
Direction-finding, 57
Displaced Persons, 96, 101, 127, 132
Doenitz, Alfred, 59, 120
Dombrowski, James, 30
DPs. *See* Displaced Persons
Dreyfus, Werner, 32, 129
Du Bois, Edward, 96

Egger, Bruce, 144n
Eighth Air Force, 57, 85
Eisenhower, Dwight D., 81, 124
Enlisted Reserve Corps, xv, 3, 23

Folkestone, 55–56
Fort Dix, 13–17
Fouron St. Pierre, 73

German anti-Nazis, 105–106
German economy, 94–95, 99
German industry, 113–15

147

German political opinions, 106–109
Given, Roland, 86
Godzevsky, Alexander K. (Sasha), 7–12, 36
Goebbels, Alfred, 60, 72, 89, 93, 101
Goldberg, Arthur (Arch), 73–74
Goldberg, Isidor, 8
Gottlieb, Ferdinand, 64, 80–83
Gourock, Scotland, 48
Greensboro, 40

Harrison, Cleveland, 144n
Hayes, Weyland B., 29
Heidelberg, 124, 127, 131–32,
Helmstedt, 123, 131
Highlander Folk School, 30
Hitler Youth, 90, 108
Holocaust. *See* Atrocities
Homosexuality, 19
Horne, John, 143n
Hospital, German military, 112
Hospitals, U.S. military, 17–18, 133–39

Industry, German. *See* German industry
Intelligence, Military, 33, 118
Intelligence, Signal, 34–35, 52, 56–58
Interrogation of prisoners, 127–29

Jews, encounters with, 65–66, 69, 103, 113, 122, 132
Joplin, Missouri, 21–23

Kallman, Chester, 10, 40
Kaufbeuren, 125–26, 145n
Kellogg-Briand Peace Pact, 3
Kitchen Police duty, 14–15, 24–25, 37
Klonsky, Milton, 32, 40
Klonsky, Rhoda Jaffe, 32, 143n
Knauth, Hans, 69–70
Kotlowitz, Robert, 144n
KP. *See* Kitchen Police duty
Kramer, Alan, 143n
K Rations, 62
Kreis, John F., 144n

Language skills, xv
Language studies, 27
Leeds, Franklin T., 31, 129–30
Lehrman, Daniel, 29–30
Lend-Lease program, 6, 7
Liège, 56, 73
Linderman, Gerald, 143n
London, 53–55
Luftwaffe, 52, 56–58, 84–85, 118; General Staff, 127–29
Luxembourg, 67–72, 92, 95, 144n; prison, 70–72

Maastricht, 78
MacDill Field, 34, 37, 38

Magdeburg, 98
Magermans, Pierre, 85
Mathias, Frank Furlong, 144n
Message Center School, 18, 20, 23, 24
Messerschmidt, Willy, 127
Military government, 102–109
Military intelligence. *See* Intelligence, Military
Molotov-von Ribbentrop Pact, 4
Monteagle, Tennessee, 30
Moore General Hospital, 136–39
Morton, Bert, 16, 19
Munich, 131

Nancy, 133–36
Nashville, 28–33
Nazi Party, 115, 124
Nebraska, University of, 24, 26–27
Neill, George W., 144n
Neosho, Missouri, 19, 21
News broadcasts, 41, 59
Niebuhr, Reinhold, 5
Nineteenth Tactical Air Command, 56
Ninth Tactical Air Command, 85
Normandy, 60–63
NSDAP. *See* Nazi Party

Office of War Information, 89
Officer Candidates School, 18, 23
Omaha Beach, xv, 60
Orders, Military, 36–37, 118–19
Orwell, George, 144n
Otts, Lee M., 144n
OWI. *See* Office of War Information

Parachutists, 85–86
Paris, 86–87, 123
Pepper, Claude, 39, 144n
Picasso, Pablo, 64
Pilot Radio Corporation, 3, 6–12
Pilots, German, 129–31
Political opinions, German. *See* German political opinions
Prague radio, 123
Prisoner interrogation. *See* Interrogation of prisoners
Prisoners of war, Allied, 91, 92, 101–102, 104, 134
Prisoners of war, German, 32, 47, 97, 110–11, 120, 126, 129, 137
Prisoners of war, Italian, 47, 135
Propaganda, 58–59; Allied, 4; German, 5, 89–90, 122
Prostitutes, 50, 51, 119, 145n
Punishment, of Nazis, 12

Queen Mary, 41–48

Racism, American, 29–30, 138–39
Railroad journeys, 17

Rape, 60
Ratner, Sidney, 35
Red Cross, 46, 49, 135
Reims, 65
Rhoads General Hospital, 136
Rosenblatt, Louise, 35
ROTC. *See* Reserve Officers Training Corps, 4

Schneiderman, Abe, 7
Schwarz, Julius. *See* Leeds, Franklin T.
Segregation, racial, 19, 34, 46, 49, 138–39
Shapiro, L. C., 6
Signal Corps, xv
Silverstein, Theodore, 82
Slave laborers, 91, 96, 100, 103, 104, 112–13, 121, 132
Social Democrats, German, 105
Socialist Realism, 11
Soviet Military Mission to the United States, 7
Soviet Purchasing Commission, 10
Spiegel, Robert, 94
SS, 111, 116, 132
Standifer, Leon, 144n
Strotz, Robert H., 52–53, 78, 81, 83, 92, 95, 145n; visits to relatives, 67–69

Tampa, 34, 38
Thefts, from Germans, 91, 109, 121–22
Third Radio Squadron Mobile (G), 53, 56–59
Tilove, Gus. *See* Tyler, Gus
Toul, 134
Training, Basic. *See* Basic Training
Troop movements, 136
Twelfth Army Group, 119
Tyler, Gus, 31

United Service Organizations (U.S.O.), 28
USO, 143n

V-1 Rockets, 55–56
V-2 Rockets, 56
Vanderbilt University, 28–33, 141
V-E Day, 122
Venereal disease, 3
Verviers, 77–78
Vint Hill Farms, 35–36
Volkssturm, 89, 116, 145n
Von Rundstedt Offensive. *See* Battle of the Bulge

Waffen SS, 91, 96
War industry, American, 6–12
Washington, Booker T., 29
Washington, D.C., 35
Weymouth, 60
Wiesbaden, 118, 145n

Yoselowitz, Harry, 30, 48, 120, 145n
Young Communist League, 36

ISBN 1-58544-299-2